*Life*STYLE

Real Perspectives from
Radical Women
in the Bible

Whitney Prosperi

NEW HOPE
PUBLISHERS

Birmingham, Alabama

New Hope® Publishers
P. O. Box 12065
Birmingham, AL 35202-2065
www.newhopepublishers.com
New Hope Publishers is a division of WMU®

The Library of Congress has catalogued the earlier edition as follows:
Prosperi, Whitney.
    Life style : real perspectives from radical women in the Bible / Whitney Prosperi.
        p. cm.
    ISBN 1-56309-812-1 (softcover)
    1.Women in the Bible. 2. Teenage girls-Religious life.
3. Teenage girls-Conduct of life. I. Title.
BS575.P76 2004
248.8'33—dc22
2004010191

ISBN-10: 1-59669-336-3
ISBN-13: 978-1-59669-336-4

N126102 • 1011 • 1.5M7

Table of Contents

Acknowledgments

I would like to thank the following people who have helped shape my life thus far. To you I owe a large part of this book.

Those who prayed as I wrote: I felt your prayers and saw them answered.

The girls of CFBC & Caliope: What precious memories I have of following Him together with you. You are blessed because you believe what the Lord has told you will be accomplished.

CFBC staff: Thank you for encouraging me to dream big. I am grateful for the privilege of serving with you.

Pastor Shook: God used you to plant in my heart a love for His Word. Thank you.

Louie & Shelley Giglio: Thank you for your investment in my life and for helping my faith to grow.

Mom, Dad & Wade: Thank you for your love and support through the years and for your consistent example of what it means to walk with God.

In working with teenage girls for years, I have become keenly aware of the lack of biblically solid, thought-provoking material to challenge this ever-changing demographic. Look no further! Whitney Prosperi delivers just what our girls need in *Life STYLE*. It is by far the finest teen girl Bible study I've seen in a long time. From topic choices to layout to spiritual insight, *Life STYLE* is fabulous from beginning to end! Buy one today for every girl you know!

—*Shelley Breen, Point of Grace*

Relevant. Practical. Transforming. *Life STYLE* is straight-to-the-heart stuff that will rock the teen girl world. Whitney Prosperi's own love affair with Jesus and her passion for nurturing and shaping young hearts for Christ ooze from every chapter. A great tool for personal Bible study, small groups, or for moms and daughters to share together. Every teen girl desperate for what really fills the soul should devour this book!

—*Louie Giglio, Passion Conferences,*
author of The Air I Breathe: Worship as a Way of Life

Bravo Whitney! Your finger has always been on the pulse of teen girls. Now you've written a Bible study that reflects your insight into the heart hunger of every teen girl.

—*Jackie Kendall, author of* Lady in Waiting

Whitney is a dear friend who has a passion to see young women seek the heart of God in every part of their lives. In *Life STYLE* I see a powerful tool for teen girls to use in their daily personal time with God. Whether they are just beginning their pursuit of God or desire to go deeper, this study encourages girls to press into the Word of God and establish Jesus Christ as the first love of their lives. I will reserve a copy for my young daughter to have in the years to come!

—*Christy Nockels, Watermark*

Finally a Bible study resource for youth girls! As someone who has been in the trenches of ministry to youth-aged girls for many years, Whitney is more than qualified to write this study. She has done a beautiful job of taking women in the Bible and bringing them to life on a level that relates to the average teen girl. I can't wait to recommend this resource!

—*Vicki Courtney, Founder of Virtuous Reality Ministries,*
author of Your Girl: Raising a Godly Daughter in an Ungodly World

Whitney has always had a passion for pointing girls to God's *better way*! She has done a great job of pointing her readers to God's wisdom—not prevailing cultural opinions. It has been said, and I believe it to be true, that we don't change the way we *act* until we change the way we *think*. This workbook is a practical tool to help girls *think* biblically about priorities, service, influence, dating, grace, forgiveness, and God's calling on their lives. Long before Whitney ever wrote this, she practiced these principles—*it was her Life STYLE*. She gives great insight into God's heart and high calling for women.

—*John Wills, Education & Family Minister,*
Sagemont Church, Houston,
Conference Speaker & Director, Song of Solomon for Students

If you're looking for a practical yet creatively interactive girls' Bible study, you can't afford to miss this book. This study is for real girls who desire a deep and radical relationship with their heavenly Father. Girls are encouraged to delve into both the Old and New Testament stories and see how God radically used women throughout His Word to make His glory known.

—*Cheryl S. Miller, Girls Minister,*
Champion Forest Baptist Church, Houston

I am so excited about recommending to you *Life STYLE*. God has uniquely gifted Whitney to minister to young ladies. Her passion and love for the Lord and teenage girls can be seen in the pages of this study. In a day when many have lost their way, this Bible study gives clear direction from God's Word about the critical issues that face young ladies in our culture today!

—*Mike Taylor, Student Minister,*
Champion Forest Baptist Church

Whitney Prosperi offers a relevant look at God's "Life Style" for girls of this generation. This passionate, life-changing study connects readers to the grace and mercy of Christ, and draws them into a lifelong love affair with the Creator of the Universe.

—*Eric Hill, Junior High Pastor,*
Second Baptist Church, Houston

Introduction

efore we begin this journey together through *Life STYLE*, I want to say welcome. I am so glad you have chosen to study and learn along with me. In the next few weeks we are going to meet 12 women of the Bible and see their stories unfold before us. We'll meet everyone from a beauty queen to a young girl who was raped. Each one of these women has something valuable to teach us. Every week we'll also encounter a modern day heroine who in some way resembles the biblical woman we are studying. Through these studies we'll cover topics such as understanding your salvation, learning to trust God with your future, and realizing that you can have an impact on the whole world for Christ. So as we start, let me challenge you to bring along your imagination, your teachable heart, and a Bible.

This study can be used several ways. You can use it on your own in your quiet time each day. If so, just set aside about fifteen minutes in a quiet place where you can be uninterrupted. You may want to devote a specific time each day to studying the lesson. You might want to pick out a colored pen to use just for this study. Maybe you will light a candle or have your favorite drink nearby.

Whatever you do, set yourself up for success. Be realistic, setting goals that you can meet. For instance, if you can't pry your eyes open in the morning, you may want to set aside time after school to work on the study. Also, be consistent. Make sure you guard the time you'll spend on your study each day. If you do miss a day, don't be discouraged. Just start again the next day.

Memory verses are provided for you to use each week. If you have never memorized Scripture before, you'll be surprised at how easy it is. Just put your memory verse in a place where you'll see it each day. You may want to write it on a card and hang it on your mirror or in your locker. You could also stick it in your Bible or purse. Just spend a few minutes every day writing out the verse or saying it aloud. You'll be amazed at how quickly that verse will start rolling off the tip of your tongue.

Life STYLE can also be used in a group setting. An ideal group size would be anywhere from two to eight girls. Each member would commit to doing six days of homework on her own and then meeting once a week to go over the discussion questions. You may want to ask an older woman at your church to lead the group time. Or if you and some friends decide to go through the study on your own, you might rotate who leads the discussion questions each week.

The key to a successful group is commitment. Before you begin, make sure each member knows that the group will last for 12 weeks. Set a time and place where the group will meet and commit to start and end on time. You may want to designate certain people to do different things, such as making reminder phone calls, leading prayer request time, or providing refreshments. Make sure that each week you go through the discussion questions, review the memory verse, and pray together. Every girl must agree to keep the things discussed within the group confidential. You also might want to write down phone numbers, email addresses, and prayer requests in the space provided in the back of your study. This book is your tool to use. Feel free to underline, circle, and star the places that speak to you. It's going to be a great 12 weeks! Let's get started.

A Note to Leaders:

Here are a few tips to help you as you lead the group through *Life STYLE*. First of all, relax and know that the Holy Spirit is the true teacher. He promises to use you as you yield to Him and pray for His guidance. With that in mind, as you prepare to meet with your group make prayer a priority. Pray each day for yourself as a leader and for each group member by name. You may want to call or email group members to encourage them and to get their prayer requests before the group meets. If you know the prayer requests ahead of time you can share them with the group as girls write them down. This may save time.

Commit to start and end the group on time. Allow a few minutes for girls to mingle with each other, but when it's time to begin, gather everyone together and start. Budget your time and be careful that you don't run over. Make sure that each girl knows the time and place you will meet and that the Bible study will last for 12 full weeks.

Encourage girls to get the most out of the study by completing their homework each week and learning the memory verse. Don't be hard on girls who haven't completed a lesson, but gently encourage them that their time studying the Word will benefit them more than simply attending the group.

Lastly, remember that God is with you each time you gather. He promises in Matthew 18:20: "For where two or three come together in my name, there am I with them."

Week 1

Understanding Salvation

Jairus' Daughter

Mark 5:21–24, 35–43

Memory Verse:

Romans 6:23

"For the wages of sin is death, but the gift of God is eternal life in Christ Jesus our Lord."

Memory Verse:

"For the wages of sin is death, but the gift of God is eternal life in Christ Jesus our Lord." —ROMANS 6:23

Celia's Story

Celia had been pretty her whole life. People would look at her on the street. Boys were attracted to her and girls flocked to be her friend. During her senior year, a famous modeling agent came to town and discovered her. He said the camera would love her. It must have, because in a matter of months her picture was everywhere from Vogue to magazines across the world. She had made it in her career and she was only 18.

The problem was that when she looked in the mirror she just saw a love-starved, abused drug addict. She saw the pain that was stuffed down under the designer clothes and makeup. She could see the little girl crying out for love. Love she had never received.

It seemed that every man she let into her life wanted something from her. They used her to make their fortunes and build their egos. She was tired of being everyone's pretty girl. She was tired of smiling for the camera when she knew she was dead on the inside.

One night after a photo shoot she put on her coat and walked out into the city street. She didn't stop until she reached a bridge. She climbed on the rail to jump. As she balanced there, an old man approached her and started talking to her. His kind spirit calmed her and she stepped back off the rail. He spoke of God's love and mercy. He told her that she could start again through the healing power of God. He told her how to have eternal life and gave her his Bible.

As she walked home that night she thought about everything he had said. His words burned in her soul. When she got to her apartment she knelt down beside her bed and asked Jesus Christ to be the Lord and Savior of her life. That night she received eternal life.

The next day she left her life in the modeling industry. She went home to her family. She started reading the Bible and letting God heal the wounds in her heart. She went from death to life because of the grace of God and the mercy of an old man.

Day 1: Life or Death

Please begin today by reading Mark 5:21–24. Ask God to speak to you as you study His Word.

What would you do if you and your best friend were home alone and she suddenly started choking? Seconds may mean the difference between life and death. Would you dial 9-1-1? Would you run to a neighbor's house for help? Maybe you would frantically cry out to God.

Jairus found himself in a life and death situation. His daughter was sick. Not only was she sick, she was close to dying. Jairus knew that every second was critical. He was desperate.

According to verse 22, who was Jairus? Circle one.
 A. A disciple of Jesus
 B. An unbeliever
 C. A ruler of the local synagogue
 D. A desperate doctor

Jairus was a very important man in his city. He was a well-known leader in the synagogue (church). But in spite of his power, he couldn't make his daughter well again. In humility, he fell at Jesus' feet.

What do you think Jairus' actions showed Jesus and the people looking on?

they probably thought Jesus is the real deal and believed more.

The fact that this powerful man would bow before Jesus revealed his great need. Have you noticed that sometimes we go through a whole day without recognizing that we need Jesus? Distractions such as boys, homework, the internet, or time with friends crowd out our thoughts about Jesus. It is so easy to think we control our little worlds, until tragedy strikes. Then we fall to our knees before the only One who controls every atom in the universe.

Can you remember a time when your world was turned "upside-down" and you realized your desperate need for God? How did you respond?

when my ex dumped me. And when my dad moved out. ~ He put some kind of comfort in my heart and said he left for a reason. with my ex there will be someone new!
P.S, i have a new Godly bf who loves me!

Jairus must have felt hopeless. Have you ever felt hopeless? Where did you go for help?

What is the best response to feeling hopelessness? You guessed it—do exactly what Jairus did. Go straight to Jesus. Bow down and tell Him your need. Jesus' response to Jairus showed His great compassion. Verse 24 says, "So Jesus went with him." He never turns us away when we earnestly seek Him.

Read Hebrews 4:16. Fill in the blanks with the missing words.
"Let us then _come_ _boldly_ **to the throne of** _grace_ **with** _mercy & love_, **so that we may receive** _mercy_ **and find grace to** _help_ **us in our time of** _need_ **."**

In this verse God chose one word to describe His throne: grace. Webster's Dictionary defines grace as "the unmerited love and favor of God toward man." Despite the fact that we don't deserve His love, He loves us anyway.

How does that make you feel? Circle one.
A. Surprised
B. Confident

C. Humbled

D. Proud

Maybe today you feel a little bit like Jairus. Maybe you are overwhelmed by a situation in your own life. You don't have any answers. Maybe you haven't told anyone about this problem. Will you come to Jesus in prayer and humility? Bring your need to Him and believe He cares for you.

Day 2: Just Believe

Let's pick up the story where we left off yesterday. Read Mark 5:21–24 and 35–36.

Just when we start to get our hopes up for Jairus, he receives awful news. His daughter is dead. How must he have felt? He wasn't even with her when she died. Maybe he felt foolish for going for help instead of staying at home with his family. Or maybe he felt angry because he hadn't gone for help sooner.

Has anyone ever given you really bad news? How did you feel?

when my grandpa died. i didn't REALLY know him, but i did feel bad for my mom.

What happened next? Jesus said something very surprising. (He did that a lot, didn't He?)

What did Jesus tell Jairus to do?

just believe

Let's look at Jesus' first statement to Jairus: "Don't be afraid." You may think, "That is an easy thing to say." Sometimes people don't know what to say to a hurting person, but this is not the case here. Jesus always said the right thing. He only spoke the truth. When Jesus says "don't be afraid," we can trust Him. Look at His words in Luke 12:6–7.

What do these verses teach us about fear? Circle one.
A. I shouldn't fear because I'm as valuable as the birds.
B. I shouldn't fear because God won't let anything bad happen to me.
C. I shouldn't fear because if God loves the birds, He loves me so much more.
D. I should only fear during hunting season.

If God cares for the sparrows, think how much more He cares for you. This passage teaches that He even has the individual strands of your hair numbered. Now that's amazing! The next time you're blow-drying your hair, remember His tender love.

Let's look at Jesus' second statement to Jairus. He told him to "Just believe."

Do you find it easy, difficult, or somewhere in between to believe in God? Why?

NO. i was young when i exepted him.

Read Hebrews 11:6. Fill in the blanks with the missing words.
"And without ___faith___ it is impossible to please God, because ___he___ who comes to Him must ___believe___ that He exists and that He rewards those who earnestly seek ___him___."

Do you believe that God exists and that He wants to be personally involved in your life? Circle one.
A. I'm not sure.
C. I want to believe.
D. I believe.
E. I believe, although sometimes I have doubts.

No matter what answer you chose, you can be sure that God exists and that He is trustworthy. Maybe you, like Jairus, need to ignore your fear and believe in God. Is something holding you back? Maybe others' opinions or your own doubts keep you from believing in Him. Will you let go of anything that keeps you from believing? Today we'll end with a simple prayer. Only pray this if you sincerely mean it.

Jesus, I want to believe in You. As I do this study, please open my heart to believe You more fully. Help me seek You as I study Your Word. Teach me and give me ears that hear from You.

Day 3: New Life

"Jesus said to her, 'I am the resurrection and the life. He who believes in me will live, even though he dies; and whoever lives and believes in me will never die. Do you believe this?" —JOHN 11:25

Let's begin today where we ended yesterday. Please read Mark 5:37–43.

In verse 42 we discover that the little girl is only twelve years old. The Bible doesn't tell us her name, but this doesn't mean she was unimportant. Just think—Jesus cared so much for a little girl that He personally visited her house. Although she wasn't someone important in the world's eyes, He still cared for her.

If Jesus cared for a twelve-year-old girl, what does that tell you about His care for you?

_____

_____

When Jesus arrived at the house, the mourners had already begun their ritual. In those days mourners were hired to help the family express their grief. It looked as if Jesus was too late.

How did these mourners respond to Jesus? Circle one.
  A. Welcomed Him
  B. Laughed at Him
  C. Ignored Him
  D. Threw rocks at Him

Picture the scene with me. He went into her room, taking with Him only Peter, James, John, and her parents. What did the disciples expect? What did her parents expect? Jairus was holding onto the words of Jesus: "Just believe." Jesus spoke to the girl and she immediately stood up. She was dead, and now she's alive!

According to verse 42, what was the response of her family?

_____

_____

_____

If this were your family, how would they respond?

_____

_____

_____

This miracle symbolizes the reason Jesus came to earth. He came so people could receive new life. This little girl represents every one of us. We are all dead in our sin before we meet Jesus. Romans 3:10 says, "There is no one righteous, not even one." Every single person has sinned. Sin brings eternal separation from God. Sounds like bad news, right?

Well, here is the good news. Jesus came to earth, lived a perfect life, and died to pay the price for our sins. He rose again, conquering death once and for all. In order to have eternal life, we must receive His gift of forgiveness. This is what makes someone a Christian. They are brought from death to life, just like Jairus' daughter.

Maybe someone has written you off, saying it's too late for you. Maybe you even believe them, thinking you've gone too far for forgiveness. Today He extends the invitation for you to receive eternal life.

Read John 3:16. Fill in the missing words.
"For _____ so loved the world that he gave his one and only_____ , that whoever believes in him shall not _____ but have _____ life."

Is there a time when you became a Christian, when you accepted Jesus' gift of eternal life? (Some churches call this a "profession of faith".) If so, when?

_____

_____

If not, what is holding you back?

_____

_____

_____

Nothing compares to the peace you'll have knowing you're forgiven by Jesus and spiritually alive on the inside. If you would like to receive His gift of eternal life, pray this prayer:

Jesus, I confess that I'm a sinner. I am spiritually dead because of my sin that has separated me from You. I receive Your gift of eternal life through Your death on the cross. Please forgive me for my sins. Be my Lord and Savior. Thank You that Your Word promises You will never leave me. Amen.

If you prayed this prayer, tell someone who will help you grow in your faith.
One important hint: You will need nourishment in your Christian life. Look at Mark 5:43.

What did Jesus recommend for the little girl? Circle one.
A. Prayer
B. Something to eat
C. Vitamins
D. Rest

Just as Jairus' daughter needed physical nourishment, you also need the spiritual protein of God's Word. As you continue this study, you will develop the healthy habit of taking daily meals from His Word—your spiritual food.

Day 4: Heart of Compassion?

"He will take pity on the weak and the needy and save the needy from death." —PSALM 72:13

What if you were walking down the stairs in your school and a girl beside you fell and dropped all of her books? Everyone else laughed hysterically and walked on by. It would be tempting to do the same. Or would you help her gather her books and get back on her feet?

Jairus' daughter was raised from the dead because Jesus went to her house and healed her. His compassion moved Him to action. Compassionate people reach out instead of looking the other way. They let God use them to help and heal.

Write your own definition of compassion.

_____

_____

_____

Describe a time when someone showed you compassion.

_____

_____

_____

If you are a Christian, you have been miraculously brought from death to life. What will you do now? Will you keep this gift of salvation to yourself or share it with others who need it? God wants to use you. Will you let Him?

Read Psalm 116:3–9. Fill in the blanks with the missing words.
**Verse 5: "The LORD is _____ and _____ ;
our God is full of _____."**

This verse describes God differently than the world sees Him, doesn't it? Most people think He is waiting to "get them." Those who know Jesus know that's not true.

Psalm 116:9 says that because we've received new life we can "walk before the LORD in the land of the living."

What do you think this verse means by "walk before the Lord"? Circle one.
A. We can live in His will.
B. He uses us in the world.
C. We live in relationship with Him.
D. All of the above.

God empowers Christians to do all of the above. As we live in daily relationship with Him He uses us to impact our world. Does that mean we go around raising dead people back to life? No. It simply means we have compassion as Jesus did. We share with others how to receive eternal life.

Does someone in your family or school need to hear about God's gift of eternal life? Who is it?

_____

_____

_____

_____

Will you share the truth with this person? Circle one.
A. Yes, but I'm scared.
B. No, I'm not ready.
C. Yes, but I doubt they'll listen.
D. Other _____

According to Colossians 3:12, what behavior is expected of Christians?

_____

_____

_____

_____

Will you act compassionately, as Jesus did? The first step is meeting someone's needs. That may mean you befriend someone in your school who doesn't have friends. Is there someone who came to your mind? Or you might volunteer your time with those less fortunate or in a nursing home. Let compassion move you to action. This is part of understanding your gift of salvation and wanting to share it.

Read James 2:15–16. Why is it so important to meet someone's physical needs before trying to meet their spiritual needs?

_____

_____

_____

Throughout this week, ask God to open your eyes to those with needs. Then respond to them with compassion. This is an important step to make as a Christian.

Day 5: Are You Shining?

"I will not die but live, and will proclaim what the LORD has done."
—PSALM 118:17

Let's look at Jairus' daughter one last time. She was a walking miracle. I don't know about you, but I have a hard time keeping miracles to myself.

Reread Mark 5:42–43. What "strict orders" did Jesus give her family? Circle one.
A. Clean her room.
B. Write an article for the local paper.
C. Don't let anyone know about this.

It may seem strange that Jesus told them to keep this miracle a secret. Aren't we supposed to share the good news of Jesus Christ?
    Jesus didn't want people to follow Him only for His miracles. Instead, He wanted them to follow because they truly believed He was the Son of

God. Jesus also had a much greater plan to fulfill and revealed Himself only in God's timing.

Do people follow Jesus for the wrong reasons today, as they did back then? List some of those reasons.

_____

_____

_____

Have you ever followed for the wrong reason? If so, what was it?

_____

_____

_____

Read Matthew 5:14–16. Fill in the blanks with the missing words. Verse 16: "In the same way, let your _____ **shine before men, that they may see your** _____ **deeds and praise your** _____ **in heaven."**

In this passage believers are commanded to share the good news.

Why do you think people keep His truth a secret? Circle one.
A. Shame or embarrassment.
B. Fear of what others will think.
C. Fear of losing friends.
D. Afraid they won't have the right words.

What can you do to overcome your fear of telling others about Jesus?

_____

_____

_____

_____

Mark 5:42 says that Jairus' family was "completely astonished." Will you share the miracle of eternal life so others can also be amazed at God's love? Make a list of five people in your life who do not know Jesus. Put this list somewhere you will see it each day. You might place it in your Bible or on your mirror. Will you commit to pray for these people daily? Ask God to soften their hearts and give you an opportunity to share with them. When the opportunity comes, take it. You don't have to know all the right words. Just tell them what Jesus did in your own life. They just may be "completely astonished."

Action Point

This week we studied about the gift of eternal life. In John 3:3 Jesus said to a man named Nicodemus, "I tell you the truth, no one can see the kingdom of God unless he is born again."

If you have been born again, set aside time to make a spiritual birth certificate. It doesn't have to follow any certain official format or be fancy. It will be a reminder of your spiritual birth to keep in your Bible or hang on your wall. If you know it, you may want to record the date you received Christ. You might add your favorite Bible verse or decorate your certificate. Be as creative as you'd like.

Week 2

Getting to Know Jesus

The Woman at the Well

John 4:4–30, 39–42

Memory Verse

John 6:35

"Then Jesus declared, 'I am the bread of life. He who comes to me will never go hungry, and he who believes in me will never be thirsty.'"

Memory Verse:

"Then Jesus declared, 'I am the bread of life. He who comes to me will never go hungry, and he who believes in me will never be thirsty.'"

— JOHN 6:35

Jamie's Story

J amie was the perfect girl. She had clothes to die for, a flawless complexion, a stick-thin body, and gorgeous hair. To top it off, she was smart, athletic, and funny. She was a cheerleader, model, and top student. She even found time to date half the football team. Every girl at her school wanted to be her—until she collapsed one day in front of everyone in the lunchroom.

Jamie had an eating disorder. She lived on 700 calories a day and worried constantly about her weight. At first it started as a simple diet. She just wanted to lose a few pounds. Then the diet became a way of life . . . and then a controlling monster. She couldn't make herself eat. Anyway, she liked the attention she got from boys and the envious looks girls gave her in the hall.

When she was in control of her eating it made her feel good somehow, like she would one day be thin enough, one day be happy. Happiness was all she ever wanted. She looked for it in popularity, relationships, activities, and even sex. Just when she felt happy, it would drift away and she would look elsewhere.

After her collapse and a lengthy stay in the hospital, she started seeing a counselor. He told her about the love of Jesus and her need for salvation. She received Jesus as her Lord and Savior and started to read the Bible every day. She learned about His unconditional love. She saw that all the ways she tried to get her needs met were based on lies. Only a personal relationship with Jesus could meet her needs for love.

Today Jamie is walking the road to recovery. She maintains a healthy weight and good eating habits. She continues to read her Bible—to drink daily from God's Word. She is still popular in her school, but now it's not because of her dating antics. Instead she witnesses to other girls who need to hear about Jesus. She has let God use her past as a testimony of His grace.

Day 1: Who Can Satisfy?

Begin by reading John 4:4–18. Ask God to speak to you as you study His Word. This week we're going to study how to get to know Jesus better. As you grow as a Christian, you will realize that Jesus is waiting to meet the needs in your life.

Have you ever been extremely thirsty? Maybe you were exercising or working outside. Maybe you were so thirsty that all you could think about was a big mug of hot chocolate. What? Of course not. Hot chocolate is the last thing you want on a warm summer's day. When you're extremely thirsty you crave pure, cold water. It's the only thing that satisfies.

Did you know that you have a thirst in your soul as well as in your body? God created us with deep needs in our souls that can only be satisfied by Him. Just as water quenches our physical thirst, God quenches our inner thirst.

Did you know you have a thirsty soul that needs God? Circle one.
A. Yes, it feels thirsty most of the time.
B. No.
C. I'm not sure.
D. Other _____

Let's look back at the woman in the story. She came to the well on this day just as every other day. She wasn't expecting to meet Jesus. She simply wanted to get the water she needed. She didn't have a shower or sink at home. Instead, if she wanted water for washing, cooking, or bathing she had to go to the well. (Aren't you grateful for modern inventions?)

This woman came to the well at noon while most women came in the morning or evening to avoid the heat. Some think that because of her reputation she came at the "off time" to avoid stares from other women. She may have felt shame for her behavior.

Have you ever tried to hide from others because you were ashamed?

If so, describe the situation and how you felt?

_____

_____

_____

Why do you think the woman at the well was ashamed?

_____

_____

_____

You guessed it. She had a reputation for jumping from man to man. Sounds like her soul was thirsty to me. Often when we really need God, we run from person to person looking for someone else to satisfy us.

There are three basic places most people go to get their souls' thirsts quenched.

1. People. This woman thought men would meet her needs. Maybe she kept looking for the perfect guy to fill her emptiness. That kind of thinking would keep her looking forever. The only perfect man is Jesus Christ. Maybe you're like her and constantly need a guy in your life to feel valued and loved. Whether you realize it or not, this is a dangerous cycle. **Why do you think we're tempted to go to others instead of God to meet our needs?**

_____

_____

_____

2. Pleasure. Many people mistake the longing in their souls for the need to get more stuff. They fill their lives with activities, possessions, and new experiences. Some try alcohol, drugs, food, or becoming super-thin. But one time is never enough. One new outfit. One drink. One cupcake. One binge. One sexual experience. It can never meet that thirst inside.

Is there a habit or action you use to get your needs met? If so, write about it here.

_____

_____

_____

3. Personal Accomplishment. One more place we look to get our thirsts met is accomplishment. We push ourselves, thinking if we could be #1 we would feel satisfied. We must look perfect, act perfectly, and have everyone like us. This cycle of perfectionism leaves us exhausted and empty.

Have you ever fallen into this trap? What happened?

_____

_____

_____

The key to getting our spiritual thirsts quenched is knowing which well satisfies.

Read John 4:13–14. Fill in the blanks with the missing words. "Jesus answered, 'Everyone who drinks this water will be _____ again, but whoever_____ the water I give him will never _____.'"

Maybe today you've realized your soul is thirsty. You may be looking to the wrong waters to satisfy. Will you bring your thirsty soul to Jesus and let Him be the One who fills your heart?

Day 2: Are You Digging?

Read John 4:4–18 again. Ask God to teach you from His Word. Did you know that your actions reveal your heart? Our lifestyle choices reflect the places our hearts look for satisfaction. This woman's history of poor choices revealed that she looked to men to meet her needs.

What do your choices show about where you go to get your needs met?

_____

_____

_____

If you've made poor choices in the past, now is the time to turn around and go another way. A wise young woman learns from her mistakes and relies on God's power to change. Maybe you are constantly on a diet, or you jump in and out of relationships. Or you are never satisfied with "good" and must be "best." If any of these are true about you, you may be looking to the wrong well.

Read Jeremiah 2:13. Fill in the blanks with the missing words.
"My people have committed two sins: They have _____
me, the spring of living water, and have _____ their own cisterns,
_____ cisterns that _____ hold _____."

This verse speaks about children of God who have turned away from God to get their needs met elsewhere.

Why do you think we do this? Circle one.
A. God seems distant.
B. We don't trust that He can satisfy.
C. We believe other things will satisfy.
D. Other _____

A cistern is a tank that stores water. If God is the best source for quenching our spiritual thirst, why would we dig other cisterns?

What does Jeremiah 2:13 say about the cisterns we dig?

_____

_____

_____

_____

Picture yourself walking in the door to your home after a hard workout. Maybe you jogged or did a mean kickboxing routine. You can't wait to grab a cool glass of ice water and a power shower. You turn the nozzle and . . . nothing! The water is all dried up. That's what it's like for people who dig wells that can't hold water. They approach a well in need of refreshment—but find it dried up.

Are there dried up wells in your life? Have you tried to drink from the well of popularity or thinness? What about the well of relationships with boys? Or thrill seeking? If so, you are probably very thirsty today.

List the names below of those dry wells you've tried, and next to each one write "DRY WELL."

_____

_____

_____

_____

When you're tempted to return to those wells, remember that God is the only well that quenches the soul. Look back at Jeremiah 2:13.

What does God call Himself in this verse? Circle one.
A. Holy
B. Father of lights
C. Spring of living water
D. King of cisterns

As we'll see later in the story, the woman at the well recognized Jesus was her only hope for satisfaction. Have you realized that? If so, your soul will find fulfillment.

Day 3: An Invitation

When was the last time you had something to drink? Two weeks ago? Two months? Two years? Of course not! If that were the case you would be dead. Humans need water for survival.

Did you know that the same principle applies to your spiritual life? If you don't drink consistently from the well of God's Word, you won't make it. The Bible is essential for growth, energy, and cleansing. As you participate in this study you are building a healthy habit into your lifestyle. Experts say that to add a new habit it only takes most people 21 days. You are almost halfway there.

Read John 7:37–38. Fill in the blanks with the missing words.
"On the last and greatest day of the Feast, Jesus stood and said in a loud voice, 'If anyone is _____, let him come to _____ and drink. Whoever believes in _____, as the Scripture has said, streams of _____ _____ will _____ from within him.'-"

What an amazing invitation! Jesus doesn't invite us to come to a church or religion, but to come to Him. The Christian life isn't a set of rules, but a relationship with Jesus Christ.

Now read James 4:8. What promise is given to those who draw near to God?

_____

_____

_____

_____

_____

God is the only one who promises to come close to you as you draw close to Him. No one else can make that guarantee. Friends and boyfriends may not be there when you need them. Family may not be consistent. Isn't it comforting to know God will always keep His promises to you?

How do we draw close to Him? The main way is by spending time with Him in His Word. This is where we listen to Him and respond back. Quiet times are also an important way we grow in our faith and continue to deepen our relationship with Jesus.

How consistently do you spend time alone with God? Circle one.

A. Every day

B. I'm becoming more consistent

C. Rarely

D. When I have time

Planning your quiet time will help you become more consistent. Why not schedule time with God as you would any other commitment? Or better yet, why not treat it like a very special date? Set the time and place and plan what you'll do. You may want to buy a journal where you can write what you learn. You might look for a Bible study similar to this one and a Bible translation that's easy to understand. Having a plan will help you succeed.

What's the best time and place for you to get alone with God?

_____

_____

_____

What can you do to help you keep your daily date with God?

_____

_____

_____

If you had a date with a special guy or a party to go to with your best friend, you wouldn't cancel it because you were tired or busy. Will you be as committed to your time with Jesus?

Read Psalm 42:1–2. How does the writer feel about His time with God? Circle one.

A. He can take or leave it

B. It's crucial to his survival, like water to a deer

C. He enjoys it

D. It's great if he has time

Do you look forward to a daily time with God like this writer? If not, don't worry. The more time you spend with God, the more you will want to spend time with Him. Draw close to Him—one day at a time.

Day 4: More Than Sunday

Please read John 4:19–26. Ask God to speak to you through His Word.

Did you notice that the woman changed the topic when the conversation got too personal?

What did Jesus discuss with her before she turned the conversation to worship? Circle one.
A. Water quality
B. Weather
C. Her relationship history
D. Prayer

When Jesus pinpointed her place of need, she immediately recognized He was not just any man. She started to ask Him spiritual questions. Specifically, she asked about worship.

In verses 23–24, what two qualifications does Jesus give for true worshipers?

_____

_____

_____

1. Spirit: Worship is to be led by the Holy Spirit. He always draws attention to Jesus. Anytime worship glorifies man, it isn't true worship.

2. Truth: Worship is based on the truth of God's Word. God looks at our hearts and knows if we're sincere or putting on a show.

Public worship occurs when believers join together. This can take place at church or in smaller groups of Christians. Private worship is simply time when you get alone with Jesus and praise Him for who He is and for what He has done in your life.

Who He is: The Bible lists many names for God, such as Father, Shepherd, and Living Water. In John 4:25–26 Jesus calls Himself the Messiah. There are hundreds more names for God throughout the Bible.

What is your favorite name of God? If you can't think of one, flip through the Psalms, where many names for God are listed.

_____

What He has done: Worship always responds to the things God has done in our lives. You may want to start by thanking Him for the gift of salvation.

What else has He done in your life for which you can worship Him?

_____

_____

_____

Worship can be as simple as singing to Him or writing Him a letter of praise. The key to worship is focusing our hearts and minds on Him.

How can you make sure you're worshiping Him in spirit and truth?

_____

_____

_____

How comfortable are you with worshiping God in private? Circle one.
A. Not very. That would make me feel weird.
B. I love to worship God in private.
C. I am learning more about what this is.
D. Other _____

You may want to find a worship CD you can use in your private worship time. The style of music isn't as important as the words you sing to God. Do they focus on Him? Remember, He isn't listening to your voice, but your heart's expression.

Day 5: Getting the Word Out

Read John 4:27–30 & 39–42.

How did the disciples respond to Jesus when they returned and found Him talking with a woman? Circle one.
A. Anger
B. Surprise
C. Happiness
D. Fear

In those days women were not to talk to men in public. In this case, she wasn't only a woman, she was a Samaritan woman. Jews despised people who came from the region of Samaria and avoided all contact with them—except Jesus. Aren't you glad that He welcomes everyone—whatever his or her gender or nationality? He has no favorites and no prejudice.

Reread John 4:4. Fill in the blanks with the missing words.
"Now he _____ to go through _____."

Most Jews avoided traveling through that region, yet Jesus chose to go there. No one made Him. He had to go there because He knew there was someone in need.

Do you, like the Jews of Jesus' day, avoid certain places because of the people there? Maybe there is a group at school you ignore. You wouldn't want others to see you talking with them.

Will you allow God to remove the prejudice from your heart? Circle one.
A. No
B. Yes, but it will take a miracle

C. Maybe

D. Other _____

We must be willing to cross racial boundaries as Jesus did. He came for all people. Like the children's song says, He loves "red and yellow, black and white." And He also came for the people who are different from you in other ways besides race. Consider how God needs to change your attitudes toward people. This woman was changed! She found living water in Jesus.

According to verses 28–29, what did she do after her encounter with Jesus?

_____

_____

_____

A woman once cloaked in shame became a confident witness. People who knew her must have seen a dramatic change. There is no explanation for that—except the power of God.

Do the changes Jesus has made in you draw others to Him? Why or why not?

_____

_____

_____

Verse 39 tells us many Samaritans believed in Jesus because of this woman. Leave it to a female to get the good news out! There is no reason to live in shame when the cleansing water of Jesus can change us. Telling others is a huge step in our relationship with Christ. The better we know Him, the more we want others to know Him.

Action Point

On day 4 we studied corporate and private worship. Today's action point will help you develop the heart of a worshiper. Grab your Bible and a pad of paper. Read through Psalm 28 one time. Now read it a second time and watch for names of God. Also look for adjectives that describe what He's like. As you notice each one, write it down on your notepad.

For instance, in verse 1 the psalmist calls God "O Lord my Rock." In verse 7 you will find two names for God. Include these on your list. Continue through this chapter and add to your list every name for God or word describing Him.

You might want to pick a different psalm each day and see how many names for God you can find. As you become familiar with the names of God you will know more of what He's like.

Psalm 113:1–3 says, "Praise the Lord. Praise, O servants of the Lord, praise the name of the Lord. Let the name of the Lord be praised, both now and forevermore. From the rising of the sun to the place where it sets, the name of the Lord is to be praised."

Week 3

Dating According to God's Standards

Ruth

Ruth 1–4

Memory Verse

Proverbs 31:30

"Charm is deceptive, and beauty is fleeting; but a woman who fears the Lord is to be praised."

Memory Verse:

"Charm is deceptive, and beauty is fleeting; but a woman who fears the Lord is to be praised."   —Proverbs 31:30

Michelle's Story

ichelle had never dated much. There were a few dates in high school, but nothing special. It seemed like she had way more boy friends than boyfriends. Guys always liked her—as a friend. They confided in her, shot basketballs with her, and took her to dances when they couldn't find another date.

After graduation she hugged her friends goodbye and left for college. She made lots of friends and became involved in several ministry and campus groups. Once again, guys never seemed interested in more than friendship with her. But she was fine with that and trusted God had a plan for her life. If He wanted to bring someone special to her, He would do that—in His own timing.

After college she applied to a missions program. She was accepted and assigned to a town in Guatemala. One month before leaving the U.S. she attended training for her missions assignment. When she got there, Jason helped her find her nametag at the check-in table. He had an easy-going nature and she couldn't help but wonder what country he was assigned to.

Throughout the training week Michelle and Jason had many long talks. They shared about their calls to mission work and how God had guided them to this point. As the week ended they exchanged email addresses and returned to their homes. One month later she flew to Guatemala, he to Saudi Arabia. Over the next two years they emailed and prayed for each other. When they returned to the U.S. they enrolled in the same Bible college. One year later they married.

Michelle always trusted God to bring the right man in His time. Instead of chasing guys she followed God. Today Michelle and Jason minister together in Asia and continually trust God's plans for their lives.

Day 1: All Alone?

What was the last "chick flick" you saw? Did it have a happy ending? Did the boy get the girl? The girl get the boy? This week we'll study a book of the Bible that would make a great chick flick. It will make you laugh. It might make you cry. It will certainly challenge the way you think—about boys.

Please read Ruth chapter 1. Ask God to help you picture the scene in your mind as you read.

How was Ruth related to Naomi? Circle one.
A. They were sisters
B. They were cousins
C. Ruth was Naomi's daughter-in-law
D. Other _____

Ruth was married to Naomi's son but became a widow at a young age when he died. She must have been devastated by the loss of her husband.

Maybe you know a widow. How has she dealt with the situation? Choose one.
A. Grown bitter
B. Grieved deeply
C. Depended on God in new ways
D. Other _____

In those days widows had little hope of making it on their own. It wasn't like today where women get educations and provide for themselves. During Bible times widows were dependent on others for provision.

Have you ever felt alone or had someone close to you die? How did you handle the situation?

_____

_____

_____

_____

In difficult situations we have two choices. We can become angry with God and walk away from Him, or we can trust and follow Him in spite of our feelings. When things get hard, are you tempted to give up? Ruth must have been, but she chose to trust God.

According to Ruth 1:15–18, how did Ruth display her devotion to God? Circle one.
A. Prayed
B. Committed herself to Him and to her mother-in-law
C. Returned to her parents' house
D. Other _____

She chose to stay with her mother-in-law and trusted God would provide for them. Instead of seeking a man to care for her, she cared for her mother-in-law.

Are your actions toward your family more selfish or unselfish? Why?

_____

_____

_____

You are probably not a widow today, but you may be without a man in your life. Maybe you desperately want a relationship. It seems like everyone else has a boyfriend.

Will you commit to walk with God and trust Him with that part of your life? Circle one.
A. No! If I wait on God's timing I won't date until I'm 93!
B. Maybe
C. Yes.
D. Other _____

If you do commit to trust God, you'll be amazed at how He will bless you. Tomorrow we'll see how God becomes the matchmaker in Ruth's life. He wants to be your matchmaker too. Will you let Him?

Day 2: Who's That Girl?

Don't you enjoy a good love story? Ruth is certainly a good one. What happens next? You guessed it—enter Mr. Tall, Dark, and Handsome.

Read Ruth 2. Think about the dramatic changes that occurred in Ruth's life. She lost her husband, left her homeland, and moved to a new place.

Describe Ruth's attitude. Do you think she felt sorry for herself? Defend your answer.

_____

_____

_____

How would you have felt in the same situation?

_____

_____

_____

In those days Jewish law permitted widows to pick up crops the harvesters dropped in the fields so that they could have food. Ruth decided to do this and happened to choose the field of Boaz, one of Naomi's relatives. He felt compassion for Ruth and instructed his workers to leave extra grain for her.

Has there been a time when God provided for your family through someone's generosity? Explain.

_____

_____

_____

When Ruth asked Boaz why he was kind to her, how did he respond in verses 11–12? Circle one.
 A. He's impressed by her beauty
 B. He doesn't want her to starve

C. He's impressed by her commitment to Naomi

D. Other _____

Boaz noticed her sacrifice and humility and admired her commitment to Naomi.

Fill in the blanks from Ruth 2:12.

"May the LORD _____ you for what you have done. May you be _____ _____ by the LORD, the God of Israel, under whose _____ you have come to take refuge."

She didn't look for a man to meet her needs but trusted God with her future. In humility, she worked hard with no idea it would lead her to the love of her life.

Do guys see your trust in God or see you chasing after relationships? Circle one.

A. I'm trusting God most of the time

B. I'm always after the next guy

C. They don't know I love God

D. They see my confidence in God's plan

When Ruth came home with a load of food, Naomi responded with joy. She informed Ruth that Boaz was what? Circle one.

A. A hot catch

B. A womanizer

C. One of their kinsman-redeemers

D. Rich

The term kinsman-redeemer meant that Boaz was a relative of Naomi's and was eligible to marry Ruth. He could redeem or rescue Ruth from the dreaded life of a widow.

With that in mind, Naomi instructed Ruth to continue to pick up grain from Boaz's field. Ruth would be safe there because Boaz would protect her. Just as God gave Ruth good advice through her mother-in-law, He wants to use your family to guide you in decisions regarding boys.

Your parents know you best, maybe even better than you know yourself, and God has placed them in your life for your protection. Do you follow their rules and advice for dating? If so, He will bless you.

Day 3: All Dressed Up

Begin today by reading Ruth 3. Ask God to teach you from His Word.

Have you noticed that everyone has advice on "how to catch a man"? Magazines all tell you something different. "Show your curves!" "New ways to flirt!" "How to catch his eye!"

Has your grandmother ever given you advice? I'll never forget the time my well-meaning grandmother dragged me to the opposite end of the mall to see a guy in a red hat flipping burgers—and insisted that I introduce myself. I somehow got out of that one, but since then I have received loads of advice on how to get a guy's attention.

What is the craziest boy advice you ever received? Did you follow it?

_____

_____

_____

_____

_____

Who is giving you "guy advice"? Do your girlfriends share their tips? How about the fashion magazines? Be careful that you always consider whether the advice lines up with the Word of God. If you do so, you'll spare yourself a load of trouble.

Did Naomi's advice to Ruth in verse 3 make you laugh? "Wash and perfume yourself, and put on your best clothes." Sounds just like us. I wonder what Ruth's perfume was called and what she wore.

Did Naomi's advice make you wonder? By our standards it sounds like Ruth was throwing herself at Boaz, but by their customs she was simply showing her need for a kinsman-redeemer or new husband. Her motives and behavior were pure.

When she told Boaz of her need, how did he respond? Circle one.
A. "Get away from my feet!"
B. He told her he was trying to sleep
C. He proposed with a diamond ring
D. He praised her character

Fill in the blanks with the missing words in Ruth 3:10.
"You have not _____ _____ the younger men, whether _____ or poor."

Have you noticed that running after boys is very in style these days? It seems every girl on TV chases her man. You may know girls who do this. Or maybe you are a girl who does this.

Do you constantly flirt with boys to get their attention? Read 1 Timothy 5:1. How are we instructed to treat men?

_____

_____

_____

We are to be so careful in how we behave around boys that we treat them as we would our brothers. God wants our motives, actions, and words to be pure.

Another important thing to watch is our dress. If you want a boy to respect you—and if you want to respect him—you will carefully choose what you wear. Just because it's the newest style doesn't mean it belongs on your body.

First Timothy 2:9 says, "I also want women to dress modestly." Don't panic—this doesn't mean you have to find the newest style in biblical robes. It just means that you determine if the things in your closet are too tight, too short, or too revealing. You may want to ask a godly older woman to help you decide what to keep and what to throw out.

Will you prayerfully go through the clothes in your closet this week? Circle one.

A. No way! My clothes are my business.
B. Maybe
C. Yes
D. Other _____

Now reread verse Ruth 3:11. Fill in the blanks with the missing words.
"All my fellow townsmen know that you are a _____ of _____ _____."

This description meant she was a woman with high morals and godly character.

Could others describe you the same way? Circle one.
A. Not a chance!
B. Possibly. I am trying to follow God in my dating life.
C. It depends who you ask.
D. Other _____

As chapter 3 ends, Ruth returns home to wait for the outcome with Boaz. He must check to see if Naomi's closer relative wants to marry Ruth before he can move forward. I imagine she walked home that day with the same confidence and peace in God's plans that she had all along. Those who trust Him know His best is always worth the wait!

Day 4: A Prince? Or Just a Frog?

Read Ruth 4:1–12.
  Boaz settles the matter of marrying Ruth with his relative. Good news! Boaz can marry her.

How did the two men finalize the agreement? Circle one.
A. Shaking hands
B. Signing papers
C. One gave the other his shoe
D. Arm wrestling

What an interesting way to close a deal. Just imagine all the paper that could be saved if we returned to the shoe-passing custom. A little smelly, but it might work.

From what you've learned about Boaz, describe his character.

_____

_____

_____

Do the guys you date or are interested in have these qualities?

_____

_____

Did you know that God is concerned about the people you date? He is just as interested in your dating life as He is in your prayer life. When deciding if a guy is "dating material," here are some things to look for.

1. He's a Christian. I know what you're thinking. "If I only date Christians I can date one of four people." While it's true that your options are limited, you'll be obeying God. He knows what He's doing. You can trust Him.

Second Corinthians 6:14 says, "Do not be yoked together with unbelievers." Being yoked together means being joined together. We must not join in close relationships with unbelievers. That means one date with an unbeliever is wrong. Why? Because one date can lead to another. Commit to only date Christians and you'll save yourself a lot of pain.

2. He challenges you spiritually. Only date someone who is growing in His walk with Christ. Is he committed to God's Word? To church? To purity?

3. He puts your needs ahead of his own. Boaz protected and respected Ruth. He wasn't interested in what he could get from her. Instead he wanted to care for her. Is this true of the guys you know?

4. He respects your boundaries. A godly guy will value your convictions. He will never push you to do something you don't want to do. He'll get you home on time, drive safely with you, and never pressure you sexually.

The bottom line? A guy worth dating is trying to be like Christ. He won't be perfect, but he will be seeking to obey God.

Are you willing to date according to these standards? Circle one.
A. If I do, I'll never date.
B. Yes
C. No
D. Other _____

Will you trust God and walk according to His Word? If you do, you'll be blessed.

> *"No good thing does he withhold from those whose walk is blameless."* —Psalm 84:11

In the space below write a prayer to God. If you are willing, commit your dating life (or if you don't have one yet, your future dating decisions) to Him. Tell Him you are willing to walk in obedience to His Word and honor Him in all your dating decisions. At the end sign and date it.

_____

_____

_____

_____

_____

_____

_____

_____

_____

_____

Day 5: God's Formula for Love

Let's finish this love story by reading Ruth 4:13–22.

God provides Ruth not only a husband, but also a son. When God blesses, He doesn't hold back. God's quotient for love: Right man + Right woman + God's timing = God's best. Let's look at the qualities of a godly young woman.

1. She doesn't chase boys. Remember when Boaz praised Ruth for not chasing men? She let him notice her instead of trying to catch his attention. She didn't dress inappropriately, flirt excessively, or rearrange her life around him. She simply walked in daily obedience to God.

2. She focuses on inner character rather than outer beauty. Am I saying that you should throw out your lip gloss? No, it's fine to look your best as long as you realize your character is more important. Are you as concerned with your character as you are with your looks?

3. She finds her security in Christ. Where do you get your worth? Is it from guys who notice you or ask you out? Is it from your looks, or a list of accomplishments? Will you let Christ meet your needs for worth and acceptance?

4. She is committed to purity. Are your thoughts and actions pure? Have you committed to remain sexually abstinent from this point forward until your wedding night?

Which of these four areas challenges you most? Why?

_____

_____

_____

How can you cooperate with God as He changes you in this area?

_____

_____

_____

Maybe you've made unwise dating decisions in the past. That doesn't disqualify you from God's blessing. It just means you can start over. You may need to take a break from dating for a while. Focus on falling in love with Jesus and saturating your mind with His Word. The more in love you are with Jesus, the better prepared you'll be to handle a dating relationship.

Why is it important to fall in love with Jesus before pursuing other relationships?

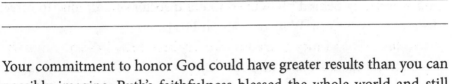

Your commitment to honor God could have greater results than you can possibly imagine. Ruth's faithfulness blessed the whole world and still touches people today. Ruth's baby grew up to be the grandfather of a very famous king.

Reread Ruth 4:17. What king? Circle one.
A. **King Saul**
B. **King Kong**
C. **King David**
D. **King Solomon**

Now read Matthew 1: 5–16. What other King came from this family line? (Hint: See verse 16).

Has God ever used your obedience to bless others? Explain.

God could use your faithfulness to set an example. You'll never know how many people watch you. Maybe you have younger siblings or neighbors who watch you. Whether you know it or not, you are a role model.

How does that make you feel? Circle one.
A. Scared out of my mind
B. Happy to have an audience
C. Nervous
D. Other _____

Will you, like Ruth, trust that God's ways are best? You can be certain God is working behind the scenes, like a director of a drama, to direct His love story for you. Will you wait on His timing?

"Wait for the LORD and keep his way."   —PSALM 37:34

Action Point • • • • • • • • • • • • • • • • •

If you're like most girls you love to dream about your wedding. The dress. The flowers. The bridesmaids. The groom! You may imagine that day 1,000 times before it actually arrives. Did you know that God knows the time, the place, and, most importantly, the man? Psalm 139:16 says, "All the days ordained for me were written in your book before one of them came to be." God has a plan for you. Will you wait for His man in His time?

Find a pretty piece of paper and a place to be alone. Then write a letter to your future husband. Tell him about your commitment to walk with God. Write about your feelings as you wait for him. Share your vow to remain sexually pure for marriage. You may even want to include a current picture of yourself. When you finish, seal the letter in an envelope. Store it in a safe place and save it until your wedding night. It will be the sweetest wedding gift your husband will receive.

Week 4

Giving God First Place

Mary, Martha's Sister

Luke 10:38–42 & John 12:1–8

Memory Verse

Matthew 6:33

"But seek first his kingdom and his righteous-ness, and all these things will be given to you as well."

Memory Verse

"But seek first his kingdom and his righteousness, and all these things will be given to you as well."   —MATTHEW 6:33

Monica's Story

Monica busily began her senior year. She was captain of the cheerleading squad, president of her class, active in her youth group, and busy with her friends. She barely had time to breathe, much less fill out college applications. From the time she woke in the morning until she finished her homework in the evening, she was active. She never felt like she could relax. There was always someone to call, something to practice for the squad, or some assignment to finish. She believed that she could "do it all."

Then one day she started to feel sick. She thought she was catching a cold, so she went to the school nurse and left school early. Her worried mother insisted on taking her to the doctor, where they found out she had mononucleosis. The doctor said, "You, young woman, need to slow down."

Slow down? How could she? She had people to see and places to go. Everyone counted on her—to help plan senior prom, to be at practices and meetings. What would she do now?

Monica missed two months of school. Under doctor's orders she stayed in bed. Her friends made it fine without her; actually, she wondered if they missed her at all. In her aloneness she dug out the Bible from under her bed. She smoothed out the crinkled pages and began to read. Each day she found comfort from the words of the psalms. She enjoyed time with Jesus more than she had any activity.

When she returned to school she made major changes. She was still involved, but she drew boundaries for herself. She protected her time with God every afternoon. She memorized Bible verses and changed her priorities. She even quit one of her favorite activities so she could volunteer with a children's program at her church.

Monica's senior year was nothing like she planned. But instead of feeling like she "missed out," she was thankful for the time to reorder her priorities. Her life has been different ever since.

Day 1: Head Over Heels

Last week we studied about relationships with boys. While that is a very important part of life, this week we'll study a relationship that is more important than any boyfriend. You guessed it—our relationship with Jesus Christ! Without it, we have nothing. With it, we have all we will ever need. As Christians we need to allow Jesus to have first place in our lives.

Begin today by reading Luke 10:38–42.

While this may be a familiar story to you, there are always new things to learn from God's Word. Ask Him to stir your heart this week and deepen your desire for intimacy with Him—and be prepared for Him to answer.

What is Mary doing in this passage?

_____

_____

_____

_____

_____

Mary was listening. Have you noticed how hard it is to really listen to someone? Have you ever looked at someone while they talked but tuned their words out? If you're like me, you know this feeling well. It happens with friends, in class, and all too often, in church.

Do you find it hard to listen when you attempt to spend time with God? Circle one.
A. Yes, I fall asleep
B. No, He always keeps me alert
C. Yes, my mind becomes distracted
D. Other _____

Today we're going to study how to listen to God. While we don't hear the audible voice of God as Mary did, we can still hear from Him. He is ready and willing to speak to us.

Read Hebrews 4:12. In what primary way does God speak to us today? Circle one.
A. Dreams and visions
B. Our friends
C. His Word
D. TV preachers

While God does speak to us through several means, the primary way He speaks to us is through His Word. God's Word directs us in decisions, tells us of His love, and protects us from deception.

Describe a time when God used a particular passage of Scripture to speak to you.

_____

_____

_____

_____

Your participation in this study shows you desire to grow in your relationship with Jesus. When you set aside time to read your Bible you take the same posture as Mary. You are sitting in front of Jesus, waiting to hear from Him. The more time you spend with Him, the more deeply you will love Him. He will begin to change you from the inside out.

How have you changed because of the time you've spent doing this Bible study?

_____

_____

_____

_____

Mary loved Jesus deeply. Can you picture her sitting at His feet listening to every word He said? She probably didn't want to miss one of His stories, jokes, or gestures. That's the way it is when we love someone. We want to spend time with them. More importantly, we prioritize time with them.

If you already spend time with God each day, protect that time. If not, will you set aside 15 minutes a day to spend in God's Word and in prayer? Schedule that time and then make it a point to show up as you would for any other appointment.

Will you commit to spend time with God in His Word each day? Circle one.
A. I will renew the commitment I already have
B. I will try it for one week
C. No, I don't see the point
D. Other _____

As we end today, ask God to give you a heart for Him like Mary had.

Day 2: Busy Little Bee

"I'm so busy!" How many times have you heard someone say that? Busyness. It's a chronic disease. Everywhere you look people are tired and hurried.

Think back over the last week of your life. How busy are you? Circle one.
A. Not too busy for what is important
B. Too busy to do the things I want to
C. I'm exhausted because of extreme busyness
D. Other _____

Reread Luke 10:38–42. How does this passage describe Mary's sister, Martha?

_____

_____

_____

Martha was distracted. Have you ever noticed that the busier you get, the more irritable you become? This was certainly the case with Martha. She actually rebuked Jesus. She became distracted by temporary things and forgot what was important.

Have you, like Martha, ever been distracted by temporary things, forgetting what really matters? If so, what was that like?

_____

_____

_____

Verse 38 says that Martha opened her home to Jesus, but she obviously forgot to open her heart to Him. Often we show up at church, youth group, or even to our quiet time, but we are so distracted that we forget He's there with us. How can we change?

Choices are the key to life. In any given day we can choose how we'll spend our time. We, like Martha, may need to eliminate distractions from our lives.

Are there any distractions that keep you from focusing on what's important? If so, list them.

_____

_____

_____

Read Luke 10:42. Fill in the blanks with the missing words.
"But only _____ thing is _____. Mary has chosen what is _____, and it will not be _____ _____ from her."

Sometimes good things in our lives crowd out time for what's best. Mary chose the best thing. Will you choose what is best? The devil loves to make us so busy that we forget to focus on the eternal. He knows that if we are preoccupied with activities, we'll neglect our relationship with God.

Now look back over your list of distractions. Is there something that needs to be eliminated from your schedule? If so, what is it and will you remove it?

_____

_____

_____

_____

What is Jesus referring to in verse 42 when He speaks of the one thing that is needed? Choose one.
A. **Rest**
B. **Sharing our faith**
C. **Our relationship with Him**
D. **Other** _____

Mary had her priorities exactly right. She placed her relationship with Jesus above everything else. Because of her wise choice she displayed peace. Jesus said that she chose the lasting investment that would not be taken away from her.

What can you do each day to help you focus on eternal things?

_____

_____

_____

A daily quiet time is one way to focus your mind even before you begin the day. Another good idea is Scripture memory. You can review your verses as you walk through the hall, practice for a sport, or get ready for school. Prayer is another way to refocus your thoughts. As your eyes see your world through the lenses of prayer, you will begin to know the difference between what is temporary and eternal. Not only will your heart change, your actions will change as well. You will become more like Mary, focused and listening, and less like Martha, distracted and bothered. Which do you want? The choice is yours.

"The world and its desires pass away, but the man who does the will of God lives forever." —1 John 2:17

Day 3: What Will I Give?

Today we'll get another glimpse of Mary's devotion to Christ. Ask God to teach you and then read John 12:1–3.

What does verse 3 tell us about the value of the perfume?

_____

_____

Mary knew that Jesus' time on earth was short. She wanted to show Him how much she loved Him.

Has there ever been a time when you expressed your love to someone by sacrificing for him or her? If so, what did you do?

_____

_____

_____

_____

This perfume was probably the most valuable thing she owned. Anointing Jesus with it showed how much she valued Him. Her love for Him was more important than planning for her future. Although the perfume may have been very valuable to her, she didn't keep it for herself.

Have you ever given up something valuable because of your love for Jesus? If so, what was it?

_____

_____

_____

_____

Do you know anyone who loves Jesus with extravagant love like Mary? If so, what are they like?

_____

_____

_____

We can't see and touch Jesus as Mary did, but we still can give sacrificially to Him.

How do you give to Him? Circle all that apply.
A. I give my money
B. I serve Him
C. I can't think of a way
D. I spend time with Him

Mary's devotion to Jesus cost her. Many believers in the early church paid with their lives because they followed Christ. Even today in many parts of the world, following Jesus may mean death. Thousands are killed each year because they convert to Christianity. In some countries, Christians are denied medical care and jobs. Following Christ may cost some people everything.

Has loving Jesus ever cost you anything? If so, what?

_____

_____

_____

Read Matthew 16:24–26. What will happen to someone who loses his life for Jesus? Circle one.
A. He will be lost forever
B. He will find his life
C. He'll receive God's blessings
D. He'll lose everything

When we hold onto our own lives, possessions, and selfish ambitions, we end up empty. Only when we give everything to Jesus are we fulfilled and free. Is there something you need to surrender to Christ? Maybe it's a relationship that doesn't honor Him, or the way you spend your time. Whatever it is, will you lay that at His feet today? As we close, pray about what God would have you do. Follow the example of Mary, who considered no cost too high to follow Christ. She truly made Christ first in her life.

Day 4: All Eyes Are Watching

Ask God to speak to you today. Now read John 12:3–8.

Has there ever been a time when you honored Christ publicly? If so, describe the situation.

_____

_____

_____

While Mary did not anoint Jesus with perfume to get others' attention, she knew it was unavoidable. In humility she entered the area where the men were gathered, knowing she would feel out of place as a woman. In that day women did not wear their hair down in public. When she let her hair down and wiped Jesus' feet, she showed extreme humility. She wanted to honor Jesus no matter what others thought about her.

Can you honestly say that, like Mary, you care less about the opinions of others than you do about honoring Christ? Circle one.
A. I would rather please Christ than look good
B. I let others' opinions dictate my actions
C. I have to protect my image
D. Other _____

First Thessalonians 2:4 says, "We are not trying to please men but God, who tests our hearts." Will you make it your goal to please God no matter what anyone else thinks?

Mary's act of worship was met with criticism. Has anyone ever mocked you for your obedience to Jesus? If so, what that was like?

_____

_____

_____

How did Jesus respond to Mary's act of love? Circle one.
A. Scolded her
B. Didn't say anything
C. Defended her
D. Blessed her

Can you imagine how Mary must have felt when Jesus said, "Leave her alone"? I imagine there are times in our lives when Jesus feels the same way toward those who mock us.

Will you take a step of faith to honor Christ? It may mean you simply pray over your lunch or take your Bible with you to school. You may speak up for Christ in one of your classes. I heard about a girl in Houston who sewed on her backpack, "Ask me about Jesus."

What will you do to publicly honor Christ this week?

_____

_____

_____

Verse 3 says the whole house was filled with the perfume's fragrance. No one in the house could escape it. Mary's love made an impact on everyone watching—and smelling. Will you leave that kind of impact on the places you go? Our lives should be so radically different that others recognize the fragrance of Christ.

"For we are to God the aroma of Christ among those who are being

saved and those who are perishing."   —2 CORINTHIANS 2:15

Day 5: Above All Else

Relationships. They enrich our lives. For females especially, our relationships define so much of who we are.

If you had to choose one friend or family member to be stranded on an island with, whom would you choose? Why?

_____

_____

_____

The good news is you don't have to choose one person. The bad news is no one person can meet all your needs. God designed our hearts with huge needs in them that can only be met by Him. When we look to others to meet those needs we ask them to do the impossible. When God comes first in our lives, He will meet the needs of our heart.

Can you remember a time when you looked to someone else to meet your needs and they let you down? Circle one.
A. Yes, it was very painful
B. No
C. Yes, I am still healing from it
D. Other _____

Read Psalm 73:25–26. Fill in the blanks with the missing words.
"Whom have I in _____ but you? And _____ has nothing I _____ besides you. My flesh and my _____ may_____ , but God is the _____ of my heart and my portion forever."

Think of the many relationships you have. List the names of some of your family and friends in the margin. Even though you may have many names written, only One promises to always be there for you.

It's critical that we keep Jesus in first place. When He is in first place we are free to love others. When He isn't, we tend to suck others dry.

In order to put your relationship with Jesus first, what practical things can you do?

_____

_____

_____

You have probably heard people say that the way to spell love is T-I-M-E. While they won't win any spelling bees, they are correct. There is no way a relationship can grow without time together.

We will end this week's lesson by reading Psalm 145. If possible, read it aloud.

David, the writer of this psalm, couldn't contain his love for God. Does it remind you of the overflowing love of Mary? Will you allow God to change you into someone who is willing to put Him first?

Reread Psalm 145:14. What does God do for those who are bowed in humility? Circle one.
A. **Notices them**
B. **Blesses them**
C. **Lifts them up**
D. **Other** _____

Jesus honored and "lifted up" Mary because of her humility. She bowed down and humbly worshiped Him. He will always reward those who place Him first in their lives. Use the space provided to write a prayer. Ask Him to help you place Him first in your life as Mary did. Invite Him to change your heart. Lastly, thank Him that He will work in you and answer your prayer.

_____

_____

_____

_____

_____

_____

_____

_____

_____

_____

_____

_____

_____

_____

_____

_____

_____

_____

Action Point ● ● ● ● ● ● ● ● ● ● ● ● ● ● ● ● ●

Set aside a time in the next five days when you can be completely alone
with God for a full hour. This may be the first "date" you have ever made
with God. Just as you would for any other date, plan what you will do.
You may want to spend time worshiping Him with a praise CD or writing
to Him in a journal. Maybe you will write Him a song or poem. You don't
need to bring an expensive gift like Mary did. Just bring your attention
and your heart. Spend the hour expressing your love to God in your own
unique way.

Week 5

Overcoming Sinful Behavior

The Woman Caught in Adultery

John 8:1–11

Memory Verse

1 John 1:9

"If we confess our sins, he is faithful and just and will forgive us our sins and purify us from all unrighteousness."

Memory Verse:

"If we confess our sins, he is faithful and just and will forgive us our sins and purify us from all unrighteousness."

—1 John 1:9

Lori's Story

The first time Lori did it on a dare. Her friend dared her to steal a lip gloss—and she did. It was so easy. The next time she stole a shirt to wear to the football game. She didn't have the money to buy it and remembered how easy the lip gloss had been. That's how it all started. Now she couldn't stop!

Each time she shopped she told herself she wouldn't steal anything—and each time she ended up stealing. She loved the rush it gave her—but hated the guilty feelings that came later. One day as she was leaving her favorite store, a man stopped her and asked to search her bag. She ended up in jail that day. Her one phone call was to her mom at work. She was in big trouble.

Looking back she says that getting caught was the best thing for her. It showed her how serious the problem had become. After serving many hours of community service, she decided to get more help. She joined a support group for shoplifters held at a local church. There she shared her problem with those who could pray for and understand her. She gradually became free from her compulsion to steal.

Lori spent time each day reading and memorizing God's Word. She asked people to shop with her so she wouldn't be tempted to return to her old ways. She overcame her habitual sin through the power of God.

Day 1: Caught!

Begin by asking God to teach you from His Word. Then read John 8:1–11.

Last week we studied how to grow in our relationship with Christ and give Him first place in our lives. This week we're going to look at some of the stumbling blocks that hinder our growth. Maybe there have been times in your life when you truly wanted to grow, but a certain sin held you back. You constantly struggled with feelings of guilt. You might even be experiencing a time like that right now. If so, this week will give you hope. God can empower you to move past this sinful cycle and into a season of spiritual growth.

Reread John 8:3–4. How do you think the woman felt when she was caught in the act of adultery?

_____

_____

_____

Have you ever been caught in a particular sin? If so, how did you feel?

_____

_____

_____

Now read Numbers 32:23. Fill in the blanks with the missing words. "And you may be _____ that your _____ will _____ you out."

Would you believe this was one of the first Bible verses my mom ever taught me? And you know what? Throughout my life I've learned that this verse is true. We can hide our sin for a while, but there is always a time when it's exposed. What a good lesson to learn early.

Have you ever pulled up weeds in your yard? If you're like me, you try to get out of sweaty work as much as possible, but you've probably pulled at least a few. Isn't it frustrating when the weeds return? You work to pull the ugly weeds, and then in a matter of weeks they defiantly sprout their heads again. Do you know why? Unless the whole weed is pulled out, including the root, there is something left from which it will grow again. That's why it's so important to pull the root up with the weed.

Sin is much the same way. We can work to stop a habit or action, but when we let our guard down, we struggle with the same sin again.

Has this ever happened to you? If so, what was it like?

_____

_____

_____

Some sins become a habit. This doesn't mean that they're okay; it just means we've grown comfortable with them. Any sin can become habitual—something we do over and over again. For some it may be gossip, cheating, or lying. Others may struggle with unhealthy eating habits, shoplifting, or sexual sins. Some struggle with worry.

Do you struggle with a habitual sin? If so, list it here.

_____

_____

_____

The first step in overcoming sin is being honest with ourselves. Are you willing to admit you need help? Circle one.
A. I'm not sure
B. Yes, I need God's help
C. No, I can handle things on my own
D. Other _____

Next we must come before Jesus. Have you ever noticed that when you sin, the last thing you want to do is pray? Why do you think that is? Circle one.
A. Guilt
B. Having too much fun to pray
C. Afraid God will be angry
D. Other _____

Just like Adam and Eve in the garden, we're tempted to hide. Will you resist the urge to hide from God and honestly come before Him? Look at Jesus' reaction to the woman in John 8. He was merciful—and at the same time truthful. Will you be honest with Him this week about the changes you need to make? If so, you will experience the freedom He has for you.

Day 2: Come to Him

Reread John 8:1–11.

Don't tattletales make you mad? Now I have to admit that I grew up as the #1 tattler on my little brother. (But sometimes he may have needed it.) The men in this story dragged the woman in front of Jesus in hopes of tricking Him. Can you imagine what this must have been like for her? She was probably not given time to dress properly before being dragged off by the tattlers. She must have been humiliated and horrified.

How did Jesus treat the woman?

_____

_____

_____

He saw past her sin to what she could become if she repented. He treated her with respect and dignity.

Does that give you hope for when you're caught in sin? Circle one.
A. Yes, I see His love
B. No, I think He will be angry
C. I'm not sure
D. Other _____

Read 1 John 1:9. Fill in the blanks with the missing words.
"If we _____ our sins, He is faithful and just and will _____ us our _____ and purify us from all _____ ."

If you are a Christian you can be assured that you will never lose your salvation, but sin can break the fellowship you have with God. It's as if you say something that hurts your mother's feelings. You can't ever stop being her daughter, but now there is a barrier in your relationship. Confessing our sins brings us back into fellowship with God. Confession means telling God we know what we did was wrong. Then we can ask for forgiveness.

When you sin, do you quickly confess to God what you have done? Circle one.
A. I do it immediately
B. No, I hope He'll forget
C. No, I ignore the situation
D. Other _____

When we confess and repent, we can believe God's Word that He forgives us. He doesn't require us to confess one hundred times with tears and sacrifices. We just need to ask once. His Word says He'll forgive us.

After you confess your sin, do you sometimes have a hard time believing God has forgiven you? If so, why?

_____

_____

_____

Although you may not feel forgiven, you can be sure that 1 John 1:9 is true. To help you remember the truth of that verse you may want to write down your sin on a sheet of paper and then write out 1 John 1:9 over it. Tear up the sheet of paper and flush it down the toilet. Let that be a reminder that God sees your sin as gone.

The enemy loves to accuse us of our old sins. You can know his voice as one that discourages you and tells you to run away from God. God's voice doesn't accuse; rather He convicts us of specific sins and encourages us to come to Him in confession.

Reread John 8:11. What does Jesus tell the woman to do? Circle one.
A. Cover herself
B. Think about what she has done

C. Offer sacrifices
D. Leave her life of sin

After confession we turn away from our sin and move forward in our relationship with God. Fellowship is restored. We are made clean. Is there a sin you need to confess to God? Maybe you have been ignoring it. Put the truth of 1 John 1:9 into practice today. Our merciful God waits to hear from you.

Day 3: Turn Back

Yesterday we studied about the mercy of God. We can always come to Him to receive forgiveness. We have assurance that He forgives us, but that doesn't mean He removes the consequences of our actions.

Recall a time when you suffered consequences for a sin you committed. Describe what you experienced.

_____

_____

_____

Consequences teach us to avoid the same sin. If a toddler touches a hot stove he most likely won't make the same mistake again. He may even have a scar to remind him: don't touch! Parents discipline their children so that the children learn right from wrong. God allows us to experience consequences for much the same reason. We learn from our mistakes and hopefully don't repeat them.

What comes to your mind when you read the word discipline? Circle one.
A. The army
B. Correction
C. Yelling
D. Brute force

Did you know the Bible teaches that God disciplines Christians who choose sinful patterns? Maybe this is horrible news for you because your parents disciplined you in anger. But God is a perfect Father who disciplines us because He loves us.

Read Deuteronomy 8:5. Fill in the blanks with the missing words.
"Know then in your _____ that as a man _____ his
_____ , so the _____ your God _____ you."

The purpose of God's discipline is to correct and protect us. His discipline develops self-control and Christlikeness.

Read Hebrews 12:5–11. From verses 10–11, what are some of the positive results that come from God's discipline?

_____

_____

_____

_____

_____

Have you ever experienced God's discipline for wrong choices you have made? What did you learn from that experience?

_____

_____

_____

_____

_____

Maybe you are grateful because God's discipline helped you stop a sinful action and led you to repent. Repentance is turning around and going another way. It is turning our backs on sinful behavior and instead making choices that honor God. Repentance is more than being sorry you got caught; it involves a life change. When we're truly sorry for our sin, it leads to repentance.

Read 2 Corinthians 7:10. What is the result of true sorrow over sin? Circle one.

A. Tears

B. Apology

C. Regret

D. Repentance and Salvation

Now read Acts 3:19. Did you see that times of refreshing come from God when we repent? When we hold our sin inside there's a completely opposite result.

Read Psalm 32:3–5. The more we try to hide our sin from God, the more miserable we become. Is there a particular sin you need to repent of? If so, do that now.

> *"Repent! Turn away from all your offenses; then sin will not be your downfall."*　　　　　—EZEKIEL 18:30

Day 4: How Do I Overcome Temptation?

Today we're going to look again at the woman who was caught in her sin. Reread John 8:11.

Has there ever been a time in your life when Jesus' words "Go now and leave your life of sin" could have applied to you? If so, describe the situation.

_____

_____

_____

_____

The Bible doesn't record what happened to this woman after her encounter with Jesus, but I have often wondered about her. Do you think she repented of her sin and followed Jesus? Was her life changed by the power of His love?

Overcoming the power of sin and temptation seems impossible when you are caught in sin's trap, but it is possible through the power of God.

When we rely on Him, He can help us overcome the strong temptations that bombard us.

Maybe there is a sin with which you constantly wrestle. It may be a destructive habit or impure thoughts. God wants to help you stand against the temptation. Will you admit you need His help?

Today we're going to look at practical ways to overcome temptation. It isn't enough to decide you won't do something ever again—because as soon as you let your guard down, you know what happens. Temptation knocks at your door, and you may open up. Let's take a look at some ways to battle temptation.

1. Realize that everyone is tempted sometimes.
Read 1 Corinthians 10:12. Fill in the blanks with the missing words.
"So, if you _____ you are _____ firm, be _____ that you don't _____!"

2. Guard your thoughts.
Sin starts in the mind. Will you guard the things you watch, listen to, and read? What about the friends you choose? Circle one.
A. Maybe
B. That's impossible
C. Yes
D. Other _____

2 Corinthians 10:5 says, "We take captive every thought to make it obedient to Christ."

In what ways can you make your thoughts obedient to Christ?

_____

_____

_____

3. Avoid tempting situations.
Are there activities you need to eliminate because they tempt you to sin? What are they, and will you eliminate them?

_____

_____

_____

4. When you are tempted, leave the situation. Or better yet, try not to get in those situations in the first place.

Read 1 Corinthians 10:13. In every tempting situation God provides us with what? Circle one.
A. Punishment
B. Guilt
C. A way of escape
D. Fun

5. If you do sin, come back to God in repentance.
He is waiting to restore and heal you. Let repentance lead you to the loving heart of God.

Battling temptation alone will get you nowhere, but relying on the powerful Word of God and prayer will lead you to victory over sin. Will you fight in the power of God's strength?

Day 5: New Identity

Aren't you encouraged that God doesn't leave us in sinful patterns, but has set us free to live righteously?

Read 2 Corinthians 5:17. Fill in the blanks with the missing words.
"Therefore, if _____ is in _____, he is a _____ ; the old has gone, the _____ has come!"

If you are a Christian, God's Word says you are new. Do you act like the new creation Jesus says you are? Why or why not?

_____

_____

_____

Many of us continually go back to lives of sin because we don't believe God's truth that tells us we are new. Now read 2 Corinthians 5:21. What is our new identity according to this verse? Choose one.

A. Divas

B. Righteous

C. Famous

D. Other _____

The key to living like who the Bible says we are is believing what God says about us. When our minds start to change, our behavior will as well.

Now read Romans 12:1–2. What can we do to be transformed?

_____

_____

_____

Renewing our minds simply means we replace the lies we've believed with the truth of God's Word. His Word has the power to free us from habitual sin.

How much time do you spend reading and memorizing verses from the Bible? Circle one.

A. Too much

B. Not enough

C. None

D. Other _____

If you struggle with a particular sin, find verses that address that topic. Read and memorize them. God's Word is powerful in overcoming sin.

The Bible not only tells you about your new identity; it tells you about your old past. Read Psalm 103:12. What does this verse teach about your old sins?

_____

_____

_____

_____

If you are in Christ, your sin is completely forgiven. The ugly sin of your past was nailed on the cross when Jesus died. You can rest in the fact that you are new and completely forgiven.

Another key to living like who God says you are is having others hold you accountable. That simply means that you tell a trusted friend or adult about the struggles you're having. Ask them to pray for you and give them permission to ask you how you're doing.

Will you humble yourself enough to ask for help today? If so, write the name of someone in whom you can confide.

_____

You, like the woman caught in sin, may have a history of sin, but God wants to set you free. Will you turn and go the other way through the power of God and the strength of His Word?

> *"It is for freedom that Christ has set us free. Stand firm, then, and do not let yourselves be burdened again by a yoke of slavery."*
> —GALATIANS 5:1

Action Point

This week we studied how Scripture can help us overcome the power of sin. Now we're going to pull out the weapon of God's Word and use it. Set aside some time to look in the Bible for verses that apply to your particular struggle. You may want to use the concordance in the back of your Bible, if it has one. If it doesn't, ask your parents or borrow one from your youth minister or church library. Find three or four verses that will help you overcome a sin you struggle with. It may take some time, but keep looking until you find verses to help you. Look up key words like gossip or lying or general words like sin.

Write the verses on an index card or small piece of paper that will easily fit in your purse or backpack. Take them out during the day and think about them. You may want to turn the verses into a prayer. For example, if you struggle with worry, you may have chosen Matthew 6:34. You could pray the verse by changing a few words and saying, "God, I will not worry about tomorrow, because Your Word says tomorrow will worry about itself." God's Word is your weapon. Will you train yourself to use it?

Week 6

Letting God Heal Your Hurts

Tamar

2 Samuel 13:1–19

Memory Verse

Psalm 147:3

"He heals the brokenhearted and binds up their wounds."

Memory Verse:

"He heals the brokenhearted and binds up their wounds."

—Psalm 147:3

Holly's Story

Holly sneaked in the back door to her house and quietly walked up the stairs. When she got to her room, she immediately took off her torn clothes and got in the shower. As the water ran down her body, she sobbed. She couldn't believe her first date had turned out this way.

She had told him "no" over and over, but it didn't seem to matter. He was stronger than she was and had overpowered her. After he raped her he dropped her off in front of her parents' house. He drove away like nothing happened.

She must have been in the shower for an hour when the water turned cold. It stunned her to her senses and she dried off and went to bed. As she stared at the ceiling, feelings of hopelessness overtook her. Would she make it through this?

Looking back on that night still gives her chills, but years later she can see God's healing hand on her life. With the help of her family and counselors she learned how to deal with the emotional pain. When thoughts of despair overwhelmed her, she turned to God's Word. Over time God healed the wounds in her heart.

Before she graduated from high school she actually shared Jesus' love with her rapist and led Him to faith in Christ. Her story amazes the people who know her, but she quickly gives credit to God for healing her and using her tragedy to bring triumph.

Day 1: Fatal Advice

This week we're going to study a subject that is all too real. If you thought the Bible didn't deal with "real life" issues, you'll change your mind after this week. God is waiting to help us through real life, even when it hurts. We just have to be willing to let Him heal us emotionally and spiritually.

Before we begin, ask God to give you a teachable heart as you study His Word. Now read 2 Samuel 13:1–19.

Rape. It's an awful word. When we hear it on the news we cringe. We pity victims of rape and other violent crimes. Even though Tamar lived thousands of years ago, she wasn't immune to the terrible hurts in this sinful world. Her story sounds all too familiar to stories from today. Maybe you or someone you know has been the victim of a violent crime. Although it may be challenging to read on, know that God wants to start a healing work in your life this week.

According to the story we read in 2 Samuel, Tamar was tricked. Amnon developed a plan so that he could take advantage of her.

According to verses 3–5, who encouraged him to rape her? Circle one.
A. His dad
B. His cousin Jonadab
C. His counselor
D. The devil

Verse 3 refers to Jonadab as Amnon's "friend," even though he was also a relative. Although he was called a friend, he certainly didn't act like a true friend. His advice was foolish and sinful. True friends help us see when we're headed for danger; they don't encourage us to pursue sin.

Is your friends' advice good advice or does it encourage you to sin?

_____

_____

Has a friend ever encouraged you to do something that was wrong? What were the results?

_____

_____

_____

A true friend will speak up when we're heading for trouble. Instead of letting us continue on a path of destruction, she'll speak the truth in love to us.

Has there ever been a time when you lovingly confronted a friend about a destructive attitude or action? Circle one.
A. **Yes, I was worried**
B. **No, it wasn't my business**
C. **No, I was too scared**
D. **Other** _____

Read Proverbs 27:6. Fill in the blanks with the missing words.
"Wounds from a _____ can be _____."

Do you have friends who care enough to confront you when you're headed for trouble? If so, their "wounds," or the things they say that hurt your feelings, will actually spare you from far greater hurts later.

Maybe someone in your life constantly tempts you to compromise God's standards. It may be time to put some distance between you and that person.

If Amnon had rejected the bad advice, the story could have ended differently. Tamar wouldn't have been raped. He wouldn't have been led into sin. If only he had filtered the advice of his "friend" through the truth of God's Word.

How can you make certain the advice you receive from your friends lines up with the Bible?

_____

_____

_____

As we will see this week, Amnon's terrible choice led to heartache and pain for Tamar as well as for his whole family. Ask God to give you His wisdom so that you know the difference between fatal advice and godly advice.

Day 2: Love or Lust

We all dream of falling in love. If you watch many movies, your mind has probably dreamed of a thousand different scenarios. It's almost impossible to watch a good love story and not long for someone to sweep you off your feet. Love is a God-given gift for us to enjoy, but we must remember that the enemy offers cheap substitutes for God's gifts. Instead of love, he leads us to its counterfeit—lust.

Reread 2 Samuel 13:1–4. How does Amnon describe his feelings for Tamar?

_____

_____

_____

The word love was thrown around then as it is now. Today the word love is often used to mask what really should be spoken—lust.

Amnon didn't love Tamar. How can we be so sure? One look at his actions reveals he loved himself and lusted after her. He didn't care for her welfare and he placed his own immediate pleasure above respect for her. In your own words, define lust.

_____

_____

_____

Now let's take a look at how the Bible defines love. Read 1 Corinthians 13:4–8a. Fill in the blanks with the missing words.
"Love is _____, love is _____. It does not _____ it does not _____, it is not proud. It is not, it is not self-seeking, it is not easily _____, it keeps no record of _____. Love does not _____ in _____ but rejoices with the _____. It always, always _____, always _____, always _____. Love never _____."

Lust is nothing but strong sexual desire for someone. It is the opposite of love. It is impatient, unkind, envious, boastful, and proud. It is rude and seeks to please itself. It is easily angered and unforgiving. It disregards the truth. It doesn't care about others. It doesn't trust God. It doesn't have hope and isn't willing to wait on God's best. It is doomed from the start. Lust tears down. Love builds up.

Based on the contrasting definitions, what do you think the media most often portrays—love or lust? What evidence do you have for your answer?

_____

_____

_____

According to verse 15, after Amnon raped Tamar, what did he feel for her? Circle one.
A. Compassion
B. More lust for her
C. Intense hatred
D. Sorry for her

Lust uses people and then discards them. After Amnon got what he wanted, he threw her out. All these years later, lust operates the same way.

Has there been a time when someone told you they loved you, but they were hiding impure motives? Circle one.
A. I can't think of a time
B. No
C. Yes, it was painful
D. Other _____

Do you recognize the difference between love and lust? It may seem hard to discern sometimes, but the true test comes when you measure someone's actions against the Word of God. If a boy pressures you to violate your convictions, he is acting in lust. If he isn't willing to wait on God's best, he is acting in lust. What should you do? Run the other way. Break up with him. End the date. Don't let yourself get caught in a dangerous trap.

The next time you hear the word love thrown around, examine what the person really means. Do they love with the biblical love of 1 Corinthians 13, or are they hiding a heart filled with selfishness and lust?

Day 3: Unlock Your Heart

Reread 2 Samuel 13:1–19. Try to imagine how Tamar felt.

What did Amnon do after he raped his half-sister? Circle one.
A. Apologize
B. Throw her out
C. Explain his actions
D. Ask for forgiveness

Describe how you think she felt as she left his place.

_____

_____

_____

Maybe you don't have to guess what she felt like because you already know. You may have been the victim of a violent crime such as rape, abuse, or incest. Simply reading about Tamar may have brought back horrible memories for you. If this is the case, know you are not alone. God saw what happened to you and wants to heal you. He cares about you. He is the only one who can heal your broken places. Will you open your heart to His healing power and love?

Read Psalm 147:3–5. Fill in the blanks with the missing words.
"He _____ the _____ and _____ up their _____ . He determines the _____ of stars and calls them each by _____. Great is our Lord and _____ in power; his _____ has no limit."

Are you brokenhearted? If so, will you let the truth of this promise saturate your heart like a healing balm? Will you accept that God cares about you, understands your pain, and wants to begin a healing work in you?

God saw what you endured. The one who names the stars knows you. He knows every scar on your heart, every fear you battle, and every nightmare you've had.

Do you believe that God cares for you and has the power to heal you?

_____

_____

_____

Maybe you've never told anyone what happened to you. You have it all stored up inside. Would you be willing to open up to God and others so healing can begin? Circle one.
  A. **No way!**
  B. **I'll consider it**
  C. **Yes**
  D. **Other** _____

Psalm 62:8 says, "Trust in Him at all times, O people; pour out your hearts to him, for God is our refuge." Today is the day to unlock your pain. When you finish this lesson, get alone and pour your heart out to God. Tell Him what happened. Explain how you feel. Tell Him your fears. Don't hold anything back from Him. He is fully capable of handling whatever you pour out.

The next step may seem hard, but it's essential for healing. Tell a trusted adult what happened to you. You may want to confide in a parent or youth leader. If you can't think of anyone to tell, ask God to provide someone to confide in. Ask that person to pray with you and to help you get further help. It may seem scary at first, but once you open your mouth to share, you will sense a load lifting from your heart.

List the person you will tell.

_____

Now make an effort to tell them today. If that's not possible, set up a time to talk with them in the next day or so.

Hiding our pain gives it control over us. Sharing it opens the doors for healing. Ask God for the courage you need to walk the road to healing. He will answer your prayer.

Day 4: Hope for Your Heart

Read 2 Samuel 13:12–20.

Amnon not only stole Tamar's virginity and innocence, he stole her chance of ever marrying. When he threw her out in the street he made her look like she was at fault. He made sure there were no witnesses to see what truly happened. As she stumbled away from his quarters, the realization of what happened must have settled on her. She probably realized that her hopes for the future were worthless now. In those days, because she was no longer a virgin, she would never marry. She would never have a husband and children.

Has there ever been a time in your life when you realized that dreams were shattered? How did you feel?

_____

_____

_____

_____

_____

What advice did her brother Absalom give when he found out what had happened? Circle one.
A. **Don't worry about it**
B. **Go to court**
C. **Take revenge**
D. **Other** _____

Although Absalom may have meant well, his advice was ridiculous. How could she forget what had happened? He treated her pain like it was something as small as a skinned knee. Her wounds went much deeper—and ignoring them wasn't going to heal her.

Well-meaning people often give the same advice to those deeply wounded. Aren't you glad that God never tells us to "get over it"? Instead He gently comforts and heals our pain.

For the rest of her life, Tamar stayed in Absalom's house. She must have felt incredible shame over what happened. One of the ironies of rape and other violent crimes is that the victim often feels guilt and shame. Maybe you know exactly how that feels. Something happened to you and you feel shameful and dirty. You may know it wasn't your fault, but your feelings tell you otherwise.

There is hope for you. The key is to make the voice of God louder in your life than the voice of your shame. God's Word says you are loved. It says you are treasured. It says He has good plans for your future. The key to turning a tragedy around is saturating your mind with the truth of His Word. Even if you have not been a victim of violent crime, you may be suffering from other shame in your life.

Do you believe what God's Word says about you? Circle one.
A. No
B. It depends
C. I do, even though I don't feel it
D. Other _____

Healing from serious wounds takes time. It may mean talking with ministers or counselors and memorizing verses that battle shameful thoughts in your head.

Are you willing to start the process necessary for God to heal you? Why or why not?

_____

_____

_____

_____

Why do you think it's so much easier to ignore our wounds than to honestly deal with them?

_____

_____

_____

_____

Tamar's rape brought horrible consequences for her whole family. Her brother Absalom later murdered Amnon. There was hatred and death in her family for years because they ignored the problem. Will you ask God for bravery to face what happened and allow Him to heal you?

Read Joel 2:25. Fill in the blanks with the missing words.
"I will _____ you for the _____ the _____ have eaten."

Although you may feel like you'll never be healthy and whole again, that is a lie from the enemy. God wants to restore what was taken from you. He desires to heal you fully. He sees you as clean and He wants you to see yourself the same way. You may feel like you'll never be innocent again— but God can do a miracle in your life!

Day 5: Beauty for Ashes

This week we've studied the healing power of God. Maybe you need Him to heal a broken place in you. While it will not happen overnight, you can be certain God can heal you. Not only can He heal you, but He can use your experience to glorify Himself. Only God can bring something good out of tragedy. Will you let Him do that in you?

Read Jeremiah 29:11. Fill in the blanks with the missing words.
"For I know the _____ I have for you," declares the _____ , "_____ to prosper you and not to _____ you, plans to give you _____ and a _____."

You may feel like your life is over now, but God is not finished with you. His Word promises He has a specially designed plan for your life. Days of freedom and joy will come.

Do you believe that God has a good plan for your life? Circle one.
A. No way
B. Maybe so
C. Yes
D. Other _____

Tamar must have felt like her life was over. According to 2 Samuel 13:19, what were her actions when she left Amnon's quarters?

_____

_____

_____

What do you think her thoughts were?

_____

_____

_____

_____

In those days, ashes were a sign of mourning. Her actions expressed the way she felt.

According to verse 18, what did she do to her robe? Circle one.
A. Washed it
B. Tore it
C. Threw it away
D. Burned it

Her robe was the type worn by virgin daughters of the king. When she tore it she may have been thinking about the loss of her virginity. She certainly must have felt nothing like royalty.

Now read Isaiah 61:1–3. This is God's promise to those who mourn. Notice what He promises to do for the brokenhearted.

Now look down at verse 3. What does He say He'll replace the ashes of mourning with?

_____

_____

Only God can replace ashes with a crown of beauty. You may feel ugly and dirty because of something that happened to you, but God sees you as beautiful. Ask Him to help you see yourself as He does.

Verse 3 says He takes away our torn robes of despair and replaces them with garments of praise. He doesn't leave us in shame, but frees us to lift our heads and praise Him.

These promises are for you. Will you choose to believe that God can heal you from the pain in your past? Years later He may use your story to help someone else going through the same thing. God can turn around whatever evil has been done to you and use it for His glory. This is exactly what happened in Joseph's life (Genesis 37). He was betrayed by his family and left for dead. Through all that happened, he clung to God's words. He later could say about his pain, "You intended to harm me, but God intended it for good to accomplish what is now being done, the saving of many lives" (Genesis 50:20).

Action Point

God's Word is filled with promises to you. They aren't just for your sister, your neighbor, or your best friend. They're meant for you. That's why it's so important to know what they are and read them often. Find some index cards or cut paper into smaller sheets. Now grab your Bible and start looking for verses that speak to you. You may want to include verses such as Hebrews 13:5, which says, "Never will I leave you; never will I forsake you."

When you find a verse, write it on a card. Find five promises, and if you find more write them out also. Read these promises often. They will remind you of who God is and what He can do in your life.

Week 7

Trusting God

Mary, the Mother of Jesus

Luke 1:26–55

Memory Verse

Luke 1:45

"Blessed is she who has believed that what the Lord has said to her will be accomplished!"

Memory Verse:

"Blessed is she who has believed that what the Lord has said to her will be accomplished!"   —LUKE 1:45

Callie's Story

It was March of Callie's junior year. Summer was quickly approaching and she couldn't wait! She planned on hanging out with friends, getting a great tan, and shopping till she dropped. Then one day during her quiet time she felt urged to pray about a mission opportunity she had heard about in youth group. So she prayed and put it out of her mind. The next day she felt the same urge. She prayed and forgot about it until the next day.

Each day in her quiet time she noticed verses about missions and God's desire for all people to hear about His love. Everywhere she turned, it seemed she heard about missions. She thought about applying to go on the trip, but then realized if she went she would miss cheerleading camp. That meant getting kicked off the squad.

One day she mentioned to her Sunday school teacher that she was considering the mission trip. The lady almost jumped out of her seat as she told her she'd been praying for Callie about the trip. The agreed to pray together and as they did, Callie changed her mind about cheerleading. She believed that God wanted her to give up her position on the squad in order to go on the trip.

Her friends thought she was crazy, but she experienced great peace as she told her director and turned in her uniform. Callie applied for the trip and was accepted. She

believed God would take care of her as she headed off for a foreign land. Although she had a fear of the unknown, God continued to assure her through His Word. She chose to believe Him and praise Him rather than give in to her fear. Looking back on that summer makes Callie smile. God did amazing things through her and changed her heart as she let go of her own plans to embrace the plans God had for her.

Day 1: Rearranged Plans

What was the best news you ever received? Were you going to have a little brother or sister? Were you accepted for something you tried out for?

Was it hard to believe the news was really true? How did you feel? Let's begin this week by reading Luke 1:26–38. Mary was a young girl, probably no older than 14 or 15. Maybe she was around your age.

How would you have reacted if an angel appeared to you? Circle one.
A. I would have fainted
B. Scared
C. Happy
D. Other _____

What news did the angel Gabriel give her?

_____

_____

_____

God chose Mary for a very special purpose. She would carry His Son in her womb, and then when the time was right, give birth to Him. Today God chooses people to fulfill His purposes on the earth. He's not looking for perfect people, but those who walk in obedience and availability to Him.

We learn from this passage that although Mary was engaged to a man named Joseph she kept herself sexually pure for marriage. Verse 27 refers to Mary as a virgin. She was committed to following God's standards of purity. Her obedience in this area showed that she would be obedient in other things.

Reread verse 28. Fill in the blanks with the missing words.
"Greetings, you who are _____ favored! The _____ is _____ you."

Mary's character and purity got God's attention. It's not that He ignores other people; it's just that He uses those who walk with Him.

Read 2 Chronicles 16:9. What is God looking for? Circle one.
A. Perfection
B. Hearts fully committed to Him
C. Virgins
D. Other _____

If God looks at the hearts in your town, would He stop at yours? Why or why not?

_____

_____

_____

_____

He doesn't look for those with a spotless past or those who are most religious. He's looking at your heart. Is pleasing Him the first priority of your heart?

God wants to use you to accomplish His plans in the world. He desires to do something unexplainable in your life that will impact others. That's what He did with Mary. He honored her obedience and willingness to submit to Him and used it to bless the whole world.

Reread Luke 1:37. Do you believe this verse is true for your own life? Why or why not?

_____

_____

_____

_____

Although she was planning her marriage to Joseph when God announced His plan for her life, she yielded to God's plans. He revealed to her His special assignment, and she willingly accepted. She still married Joseph, but also became the mother of Jesus.

According to verse 38, how did she respond?

_____

_____

_____

You may have a plan for your life all mapped out. While there is nothing wrong with planning, our lives must be constantly available to what God has for us. When we walk obediently with Him we can be assured He'll reveal His will to us day by day. Are you flexible and available to His will when He speaks to you? Will you surrender your plans to Him so that He can use you to accomplish His purposes in your life? His plans are always better than those we make for ourselves.

> _"No eye has seen, no ear has heard, no mind has conceived what God has prepared for those who love him."_
>
> —1 CORINTHIANS 2:9

Day 2: Life Coach

Let's pick up the story where we left off yesterday. Read Luke 1:39–45. Can you imagine how Mary must have felt on the journey to visit her cousin Elizabeth? She was probably filled with excitement, questions, and a little fear of the unknown.

How would Elizabeth's greeting have affected Mary?

_____

_____

_____

_____

When God is working in our lives He often uses those older in the faith to encourage and strengthen us. They give us guidance and wisdom when we face new challenges.

Has God used an older believer to help you in your Christian walk? If so, who was it?

_____

_____

_____

Those who have walked before us often have a better perspective than we do. They have walked with God longer and better understand His ways. Their wisdom comes from time invested in God's Word.

Someone older who teaches us how to become a more fully devoted follower of Christ is referred to as a mentor. The Bible gives several examples of mentor relationships. There was Naomi and Ruth. Elijah and Elisha. Paul and Timothy. Titus 2:4 says that older women are to "train the younger women."

Do you see need for a mentor in your own life? Circle one.
A. No way
B. Yes
C. I'm not sure
D. Other _____

A mentor can be anyone older in the faith. She can be a youth minister, parent, older student, or neighbor. A good mentor has walked with God longer than you have and is someone of the same sex. She is willing to regularly meet with you for Bible study and prayer. She may be someone who takes you with her to minister to others.

Just as a sports coach teaches us the basics, a mentor for our spiritual lives helps us grow spiritually. We can learn by watching her life up close.

Why do you think a mentoring relationship is so valuable?

_____

_____

_____

Reread Luke 1:43. What did Elizabeth's words confirm to Mary? Circle one.

A. She was carrying God's Son

B. She was pregnant

C. She was going to be rich

D. Other _____

God uses mentors in our lives to confirm what He says to us. They never contradict His Word; rather, they reinforce what it says.

Maybe you need a mentor in your own life. If so, begin praying that God would bring you a mentor. Next, be open to His answer. It may not be someone you expect. She may be an elderly lady in your church or a friend of your mother's. Maybe a college student you know would mentor you.

List some people you'll pray about asking to mentor you. After you've prayed over this list, consider asking one of them to be your mentor. She may have been waiting for such an opportunity.

_____

_____

_____

Day 3: Be Blessed

Reread Luke 1:39–45.

Fill in the blanks with the missing words from Luke 1:45:
"_____ is she who has _____ that what the Lord has _____ to her _____ be _____ !"

Would you describe yourself as someone who believes what God says? Circle one.

A. Sometimes

B. Not so much

C. Yes

D. Other _____

How can you tell what you or someone else truly believes? The true test of belief is actions. Do your actions line up with God's Word? Or do they contradict what His Word teaches? It's easy to say we believe something, but the truth is revealed in how we act.

Do your actions show that you believe what God says in His Word? Explain your answer.

_____

_____

_____

Read Romans 10:17. According to this verse, how do we grow in our faith? Circle one.
A. Trying harder
B. Attending church
C. Reading the Bible
D. Fasting

The more time we spend in God's Word, the more faith we'll have. Our belief in Him will grow and we'll start to act according to His Word.

Reread Luke 1:45. Do you want this verse to describe you? If so, keep your commitment to read the Bible every day. Memorize it. Think about it. Let it change who you are.

Maybe you struggle to believe that God really loves you and has a plan for your life. Will you find verses that tell you about His love for you and plans for your life? Read those verses several times a day. Pray over those verses. You'll find that over time you'll start to trust that God really can accomplish His work in you.

The enemy wants to keep us from believing God. He doesn't want us to believe that God is good and that He loves us.

Why do you think it's so important that we trust what God says?

_____

_____

_____

God's promises never fail. His Word is true. Those who believe in His Word and unfailing love will be blessed beyond their wildest dreams. You can trust Him!

Day 4: More Than Words

How many words do you think you speak each day? Think of the conversations you have with your friends, at your school, with your family, and on the phone. Girls especially seem to always have something to say.

Out of all the words you speak in a day, how many of those words praise God? Ouch! We often spend much more time talking about trivial things than we do praising the eternal God of the Universe.

Do you remember Mary's exclamation of praise from our reading this week? Review Luke 1:46–55.

List some of the things she praises God for in this passage.

_____

_____

_____

Now read Psalm 148. What is the theme of this psalm?

_____

_____

_____

Do you set aside time each day to express your praise to God? Circle one.
A. Rarely
B. Never
C. Yes, I do
D. Other _____

List some things that God has done in your life for which you could praise Him.

_____

_____

_____

Now read 1 Peter 2:9. According to this passage, what is your purpose? Circle one.
A. To witness
B. Be perfect
C. Praise God
D. Learn the Bible

Think back over the last week. Did you fulfill your created purpose? Why or why not?

_____

_____

_____

_____

Developing a heart that praises God takes time. It doesn't come to us naturally, but comes as we set aside time each day to praise God.

Did you know that the sweetest times you can have with the Lord shouldn't be in church or your youth group meeting? They can be in the private moments when you express your love to God. They can be while you take a walk, sit on your bed, or drive in your car.

When we praise God we not only fulfill our created purpose, we take our eyes off of ourselves and put them where they're supposed to be. We focus on God and tell Him that we trust Him with our lives. We think about His goodness to us. We express our love to Him. Praise changes us from self-centered people into God-focused people.

Would you consider setting aside time each day to praise God for the things He has done in your life? You may want to do it when you have your quiet time or even at a different time. Thank Him for the breath He gave you and the mind you have. Thank Him for the specific prayers He has answered. Thank Him for how He has worked in your life. There are so many things to praise God for, there aren't enough hours in the day to list them all.

Would you be willing to set aside time each day to focus on praising God? If so, when will you do it?

_____

_____

_____

The more time you spend praising God, the more naturally it will come to you. You'll develop a heart like Mary's, where your first response in any situation will be praise.

Day 5: A Matter of Trust

Can you imagine being Mary? God used prophets and kings throughout Israel's history, but He called Mary to a task unlike any before. Not one of those men bore the Son of God in their own bodies. Not one of them raised God's Son and fed Him breakfast everyday. Her calling was truly one of a kind.

Similarly, God has something so unique for your life that you couldn't dream it if you tried. You won't be called to do what Mary did, but nonetheless He has a specific part for you to play in history. You were created for a purpose that He knows and will reveal to you as you follow Him.

Read Psalm 139:1–16.

You may not have given much thought to when you were in your mother's womb. You obviously can't remember it. But God can. He remembers forming your nose, your eyes, your little fingers and toes. He recalls every detail. Even before you made your grand entrance into the world, He had plans for your life.

How does that make you feel?

_____

_____

_____

Maybe you think you were an "accident" and that no one really wanted you. You might not think you have special talents or skills; but God created you to be His masterpiece.

Read Psalm 139:14. Fill in the blanks with the missing words.
"I _____ You because I am _____ and _____ made; Your works are _____ , I know that full well."

Do you believe this verse is true? Why or why not?

_____

_____

_____

You might need some convincing about this verse. If so, write it on your mirror this week. Let it be a reminder that although you may not look like a supermodel, you are God's super creation. He makes no mistakes!

What do we learn about God's plans for us from verse 16? Circle one.
A. He throws them together when He needs to
B. They were planned long ago
C. What plans?
D. Other _____

According to what you've learned about God throughout this study, are you willing to trust Him and the plans He has for your life? Why or why not?

_____

_____

_____

_____

Will you, like Mary, trust God fully, no matter what comes? Circle one.
A. **No way**
B. **Yes**
C. **Possibly**
D. **Other** _____

If Mary would have scripted her life, you can bet she never would have dreamed what God had for her. It's the same way with you. Although having a plan isn't wrong, we must be willing to surrender it to Him if He asks us to. Trusting Him is better than sticking with our own plans.

Action Point

Have you ever written a script for your life? Do you dream about what you want for the future? Your job? When you'll get married? Who you'll marry? Where you will live? We all have a picture of what we want our lives to turn out like someday. Some of us dream so much that we can almost see the pictures before our very eyes. Others of us may be a little scared to dream because we fear disappointment.

Write down a list of the dreams you have for your life. Where do you want to go to college? What activities will you be involved in? What do you want to be when you grow up? What kind of man do you want to marry? What kind of wedding do you want? How many children? Where do you want to live? Dream big. Nothing is off limits. Take time now to finish your list of dreams before you read any further.

Next, with your list in front of you, write a prayer under all these dreams. Tell God that you lay these dreams and ambitions before Him. Tell Him that He can fulfill what He wants to in your life and can withhold what He wills. Tell Him that your plans can be altered. Your dreams are not as important as His will for your life.

Some people think that when they surrender their lives to God He will make them miserable, but that's not the case at all. He is actually better at scripting our lives than we ever could be. He may choose to fulfill some, many, or all of those dreams—or none of them. But you can trust Him. Will you lay your life and plans down before Him today? Will you believe that He knows what is best for you?

Week 8

Accepting Your Purpose

Esther

Esther 1–10

Memory Verse

Ephesians 2:10

"For we are God's workmanship, created in Christ Jesus to do good works, which God prepared in advance for us to do."

Memory Verse:

"For we are God's workmanship, created in Christ Jesus to do good works, which God prepared in advance for us to do." —EPHESIANS 2:10

Paige's Story

Life was good. Paige had just been elected vice president of the student council. She suddenly had many new friends who were popular and influential. She even had a hot date for the homecoming dance. Her school year was off to a good start—until the student council's second meeting.

At that meeting she learned about a group of students who had been targeting special needs students on the school campus. This group was pulling pranks on them, stealing things out of their lockers, and tripping them in the lunchroom. When Paige heard what was going on, she was shocked. How could her fellow students be so mean?

She stood up in the middle of the meeting and asked what would be done about the situation. The president shrugged her shoulders and many others just looked back at Paige with smirks on their faces. One guy said that it didn't seem to be their business. Another girl said that she found some of the pranks to be quite funny. Paige was appalled. She had never really been one to stand up for others before, but she knew that God placed her in this position for a reason.

That evening as she tried to do her homework, she couldn't get the bullying out of her head. She wrote a letter to her school paper and drew up some plans to start an anti-bullying campaign in her school. She guessed that when she brought her plans before the student council they would laugh, but she didn't care. She was determined to take a stand.

Paige did encounter some opposition in the student council, but for the most part she convinced the members to stand against bullying in their school. Over the next few weeks the students who had bullied were punished and the students who had been victimized were safe. Paige made a difference in her school because she had the courage to stand up for what was right.

Day 1: Rags to Riches

This week we're going to study a true story that would make a great movie! It has suspense, betrayal, love, hatred, murder, and a beautiful queen. What more can you ask for? Read Esther chapters 1 and 2 today. Ask God to help you picture the characters in your mind as you read. You'll see that, as young women of God, we need to accept the purpose God has for us, just as Esther did.

A long time ago, when Esther lived, women had very few rights. Queen Vashti might have been one of the first women to stand up for her rights, but it didn't get her very far.

What happened to her when she refused to come when her husband called her?

_____

_____

_____

Have you ever been excluded from a position because of a stand you took? If so, explain.

_____

_____

_____

_____

Reread Esther 2:2–4. Describe the plan for finding a new queen.

_____

_____

_____

It sounds like something from a reality TV show or beauty contest, doesn't it? Did you notice they even had beauty treatments back then? I wonder if they got highlights and facials.

In chapter 2 we meet Esther, the star of this drama. From Esther 2:7–11, what do we find out about Esther?

_____

_____

_____

She was just a common girl. She came from a normal Jewish family. No one would have expected much from her. She was an orphan who had been adopted by her cousin Mordecai. She probably didn't come from a rich family.

It's important to remember that God doesn't look at outside things when choosing people to use for His purposes in this world. He looks for willing hearts. He uses normal people and displays His mighty power through their lives.

Read 1 Corinthians 2:4–5. Fill in the blanks with the missing words. "My _____ and my preaching were not with _____ and persuasive words, but with a demonstration of the _____ power, so that your _____ might not rest on _____ _____ , but on God's _____ ."

According to verse 17, what happened to Esther? Circle one.
A. She was killed
B. She was made queen
C. She was banished
D. She got a pedicure

Can you imagine how she must have felt? She went from a "nobody" who was an orphan being raised by her cousin to a queen. How would you have felt? Circle one.

A. **Surprised**
B. **Overwhelmed**
C. **Scared**
D. **Other** _____

Esther obeyed her cousin's orders to keep her Jewish roots a secret. Esther 2:20 says, "She continued to follow Mordecai's instructions as she had done when he was bringing her up." Even though she was thrust into a new position, she still followed his advice. She was trustworthy. Esther showed that no matter what happened to her, she had character and dignity. She valued doing the right thing over doing what was easy. Tomorrow we'll see how she handled her new position as queen. It wasn't all beauty treatments and bon-bons. She had some pretty big challenges ahead of her.

Day 2: Deadly Plot

Isn't it just like life? When things start going smoothly something comes up that challenges us in new ways. That's what happened to Esther. Pick up reading about Queen Esther in chapters 3–4.

As chapter 3 unfolds, we meet the bad guy. Haman was power-hungry and, to make matters worse, he was second in command just under the king. He developed a deep hatred for Mordecai, Esther's cousin.

Why? Circle one.
A. **Political disagreements**
B. **A debt owed**
C. **Mordecai wouldn't bow to him**
D. **Other** _____

In Persia, kings and officials were considered divine, like a god. Mordecai wouldn't kneel before him and acknowledge him as a god because he only worshiped the true God. He took a stand for what was right. For this reason, wicked Haman plotted not only his destruction, but also the extinction of all Jews.

Mordecai obeyed the authorities placed over him as God commanded—unless those authorities commanded something that went against God's Word.

Read Acts 5:29. Fill in the blanks with the missing words.
"We must _____ God rather than _____ !"

Has there ever been a time when you had to choose between obeying God or obeying man? If so, describe the situation.

_____

_____

_____

Unless something changed, what would Haman's evil plot mean for Esther?

_____

_____

_____

When she found out about the plans from her cousin, Esther realized she and her people would be destroyed if someone didn't act. Mordecai told her that God had placed her in the position as queen for this very moment. She could rescue her people if she courageously went before the king. Read Esther 4:14.

What does Mordecai tell Esther about God's timing and her position?

_____

_____

_____

"For such a time as this." Those words must have rung in her ears. Have you ever thought about the fact that God has placed you where you are for such a time as this? What positions of influence are you in? What

clubs or activities in school? What family? What circle of friends? These aren't accidents. God has strategically put you where He wants you in order to use you. He has a purpose for you every day.

List the positions of influence where God has placed you.

_____

_____

_____

Esther knew that to approach the king without being invited could mean she would die. Standing up for her people meant risking her life.

According to verse 16, what was her attitude about the risk?

_____

_____

_____

Esther valued doing what was right over her own life. What about you? Do you trust God enough to obey Him in the positions of influence He has given you? He may be calling you to speak as a witness for Him. Maybe He wants to use you to start a prayer ministry at your school.

Will you let Him use you in the areas He has placed you in? Circle one.
A. I'll think about it
B. No
C. Yes
D. Other _____

Will you, like Esther, follow God even when you don't know what the outcome will be?

Day 3: Behind the Scenes

Do you remember Esther's words in the passage where we left off yesterday? "If I perish, I perish." Her faith in God drove her to action on behalf of the Jewish people. Continue Esther's story by reading chapters 5–6. Ask God to teach you as you read from His Word.

When Esther entered the king's chambers how did he respond?

_____

_____

_____

She risked her life by entering uninvited, but her courage paid off. He was happy to see her. She began the first part of her plan to save her people from destruction.

Esther wasn't afraid to get involved when she saw injustice. She wasn't content to shrug her shoulders and ignore the problem. Instead, she acted boldly.

When you see injustice and can make a difference, do you get involved? Circle one.
A. What can I do?
B. No, I let someone else
C. Yes, I want to make a difference
D. Other _____

Esther's example shows us how to make a difference. The first thing she did was go to God in prayer. At the end of chapter 4 we see that she fasted and prayed for three days before she did anything. She asked the Jews to fast and pray for her to have wisdom. After she consulted God she counted the cost and acted boldly.

What evil plans did Haman plot to do, according to Esther 5:12–14? Circle one.
A. Kidnap Esther
B. Stab Mordecai

C. Hang Mordecai

D. Other _____

Haman may have devised wicked plans, but God was ultimately in control. The very night that Haman planned Mordecai's death, the king couldn't sleep.

According to 6:1–2, what did he read about in his sleepless night?

_____

_____

_____

Haman was ordered by the king to honor the very person he planned to kill. His evil heart must have hated every second.

As chapter six ends, things could go either way for Mordecai and his fellow Jews. Haman is still plotting their destruction, but we can see that God is working behind the scenes. It wasn't an accident that the king just happened to read about Mordecai's heroic act. Neither was it an accident that Esther was chosen queen.

Although God was in control, Mordecai and Esther still had the choice of whether or not they would act. It's hard to understand, but even though God is in control of the whole universe, He invites us to take part in His plans. We can choose whether or not to step out in faith. God chooses to act through those who are available to Him. Esther was willing. Are you? Maybe someone is being bullied at your school and you need to stand up for the victim.

Is there a situation in your school or community where God is calling you to act? If so, what is it and what will you do?

_____

_____

_____

_____

_____

Esther acted in faith. Faith is simply doing the right thing while trusting God to work it out for the best. As we close, write a prayer asking God to help you walk in faith in the situations He has placed you in.

Day 4: Perfect Plan

Continue reading Esther's story in chapters 7–8.

Justice is done! Haman's evil plot is exposed, and instead of hanging Mordecai, Haman is sentenced to hang on those very gallows. The Bible warns that when we try to trap another, we often fall victim to that trap ourselves.

Read Proverbs 26:27. Fill in the blanks with the missing words.
"If a man _____ a pit, he will _____ into it; if a man rolls a _____ , it will roll _____ on him."

According to Esther 8:2, what did the king give Mordecai? Circle one.
A. His signet ring
B. Mordecai's choice of land
C. His crown
D. A death sentence

The king's act symbolized that Mordecai was appointed the new prime minister. Mordecai's faithfulness was rewarded by the king and by God. While earthly rewards are not always guaranteed, obedience has positive results.

Has there ever been a time when you were obedient to God and were blessed because of it? If so, describe the situation.

_____

_____

_____

The Jews were spared because of Esther's courage. But ultimately they were saved because of God's mercy. He saw their situation and acted in justice to spare them. Although God's name is never mentioned in the Book of Esther, we can see His hand at work through each situation.

List some of the ways God worked to spare the Jews.

_____

_____

_____

You can be assured that just as there weren't any accidents in Esther's life, there are no accidents in yours. You are where you are because God has placed you there. He has worked out the events of your life in order to prepare you for the future. His will is always accomplished, but we have the choice of whether we will allow Him to use us or not.

Remember the words of Esther's cousin Mordecai when he said, "For if you remain silent at this time, relief and deliverance for the Jews will arise from another place, but you and your father's family will perish. And who knows but that you have come to royal position for such a time as this?" (Esther 4:14).

Job 42:2 describes God's plans: "I know that You can do all things; no plan of yours can be thwarted."

God is at work in the world. Will you join Him? Maybe you can think of a situation where you didn't allow Him to use you in the past.

Will you commit to obey Him in the future as He works through you to impact the world? Circle one.
A. Maybe
B. I'm not sure
C. Yes
D. Other _____

Tomorrow we'll see how Esther's drama comes to an end. Until then, stay available to Him.

Day 5: More Than Just a Pretty Face

There is no limit to what God can do through one person who is fully surrendered to Him. Esther's life certainly proves that. Finish her story by reading chapters 9–10.

According to Esther 9:1–5, what happened on the day the Jews were supposed to be slaughtered?

Haman's law decreed that anyone could kill the Jews and steal their property. Because the king had signed this order and no order of the king could be overturned, Mordecai wrote a new law that gave the Jews permission to fight in self-defense.

What was the name of the annual celebration declared because of Esther's bravery and the Jews' victory? Circle one.

A. Esther appreciation day

B. E-day

C. Thanksgiving

D. Purim

Esther was more than just a pretty face. While there's nothing wrong with beauty, focusing too much attention on outward appearance can distract us from what's really important. Let's take a look at some of the qualities Esther possessed that made her a great role model.

1. She valued obedience more than comfort.
   How was this displayed in her life?

_____

_____

_____

2. She sought wisdom.
Not only did she listen to the advice of her cousin and the servant in the palace, most importantly she sought God's wisdom.

How open are you to the advice of others and to the direction of God? Circle one.

A. Ready to hear
B. Not open at all
C. I listen sometimes
D. Other _____

3. She cared more for others than for saving her own neck.
"Look out for #1" is a popular slogan in our culture. It's so easy to just step on others to get what we want. But Esther cared for those who couldn't help themselves and risked her own life to save them.

4. She was available to God to be used in His world.

Do you see a bigger purpose for your life than just going to school and being happy? Are you willing to speak up so that others will be saved?

_____

_____

_____

Do you, like Esther, focus more on your inner character qualities than on outer beauty? One will last forever, the other fades away.

> *"Charm is deceptive, and beauty is fleeting; but a woman who fears the Lord is to be praised."* —PROVERBS 31:30

Which of these character qualities will you focus on allowing God to develop in you in the coming week?

_____

_____

_____

Because of Esther's godly character, God raised her to an influential position. She went from being a nobody to a queen and didn't forget about what was important. All too often, when we find success or status we ignore our pasts. But she knew that God had placed her in that position because He wanted her to serve Him. Just like Esther, He wants to use you. Are you yielded and available? The King is waiting.

Action Point

As we've studied this week, God wants to use you where He has placed you. He has a purpose for you, wherever you are and whatever you do. Will you accept His purpose for you?

Make a list of every area in your life where you have influence. You may want to list your family, your classes, and your extracurricular activities. Make sure you think of each place where you have been strategically placed.

Now think of ways that you can stand up for Christ in each of those areas. Write out your ideas and then pray over your list. As you go about your week, think about the things that God may want to do through you. And be open to new ideas. He just may have placed you in those situations "for such a time as this."

Week 9

Becoming a Leader

Miriam

Exodus 2:1–10, 14:21–31 & 15:20–21;
Numbers 12:1–15

Memory Verse

1 Timothy 4:12

"Don't let anyone look down on you because you are young, but set an example for the believers in speech, in life, in love, in faith and in purity."

Memory Verse:

"Don't let anyone look down on you because you are young, but set an example for the believers in speech, in life, in love, in faith and in purity."

—1 Timothy 4:12

Brianna's Story

Almost her whole life people told Brianna how wonderful she was. She was well respected in school and popular in her youth group. That's why it wasn't a surprise when she was asked to serve on the summer leadership team at church. She would teach younger children in the church and help plan events for her youth group.

The summer began well. She carried out all of her duties just as she was told. The children loved her, and her youth ministers listened to her creative ideas. She received constant praise from the leadership, and after a while she started to believe that they couldn't operate without her.

The Bible says that pride goes before a fall, and unfortunately that's what happened to Brianna. One day she was on the phone with her best friend in her little office at the church. After a while she began talking about her youth minister and some of the youth leadership. "Their ideas are so lame. I don't know why they don't put me in charge of more. Things would go much better if they listened to me."

About that time, her youth minister walked in to speak with her. He didn't mean to hear her conversation, but he heard it nonetheless. She was caught in the very act of criticizing him. She quickly ended the phone conversation and started to explain.

He listened to her for a minute and then told her that he was disappointed in her actions and would give her a week off to think about what she had done. It didn't matter where she was that week—at the pool or with her friends. She couldn't shake the feelings of regret she had. If only she had thought before she'd spoken.

When a week was up she headed back to the office unsure of how things would work out. The youth staff greeted her warmly and told her they had forgiven her and would like her to be more careful with her words in the future. It took some time to build back the trust level between Brianna and her youth minister, but overall she learned a valuable lesson of respect—and God's amazing grace!

Day 1: Dodging Crocodiles

This week we're going to meet an amazing woman of God. We'll follow her from girlhood all the way to her death. We'll see her at her best as a strong leader and at her worst when God disciplines her. Her story begins in Egypt during a dark time for the Hebrews. Read Exodus chapter 1 to see the kind of culture she was growing up in.

If you were a young Hebrew girl growing up in Egypt, how would you have felt?

What order did Pharaoh give in verse Exodus 1:22? Circle one.
A. Taxes must be paid
B. Hebrews must leave the country
C. Baby boys must be killed
D. Baby girls must be killed

As you continue reading Exodus 2:1–10 you'll meet Miriam. Chances are you've heard of her famous brother, but maybe you have never studied about her. Miriam was Moses' sister. If not for her he would have died long before becoming a household name.

According to Exodus 2:4, what was Miriam's assignment?

_____

_____

_____

Picture young Miriam with me. She must have crouched down in order to avoid being seen by the Egyptians. If you know anything about the Nile River, you know that she had to watch out for crocodiles. She had a big job for a little girl.

Have you ever been in charge of someone younger than you, such as a brother, sister, or child you babysit? If so, how seriously did you take the task? Circle one.

A. I was casual

B. I was nervous

C. I didn't think about it

D. Other _____

Miriam was a quick-thinking young woman. When the princess found the baby in the basket, what did Miriam do?

_____

_____

_____

Do you think she was scared as she approached the Egyptian princess? Do you think the princess was suspicious of Miriam? We don't know the answers to these questions, but we do know that Miriam took the opportunity God gave her. She didn't let fear of what could happen hold her back. She offered to find someone to nurse the baby, and when the princess agreed, Miriam brought Moses' mother. Because of Miriam's courage, Moses' little life was spared. And to top it off, his mother was paid to care for him.

What would have happened if Miriam had been goofing off instead of following her mother's instructions? Her obedience paid off.

Are you quick to obey your parents when they ask you to do something?

_____

_____

_____

Have you ever been assigned a scary task but then seen God work it out for the best? Describe what happened.

_____

_____

_____

_____

_____

Miriam trusted God to take care of her and her little brother Moses. She took her role of big sister seriously. Do you do the same? Your younger siblings and neighbors are watching you. Where are you leading them?

Day 2: Follow Me

Now we'll see Miriam many years later. She is no longer the little girl at the Nile River, but she still has many of the same qualities. Read Exodus 14:21–31.

What significant event occurred?

_____

_____

_____

God delivered His people from the fierce oppression of the Egyptians. God's people not only walked out of Egypt, they walked right through the Red Sea—on dry land. The wicked Egyptians weren't so lucky. As they pursued God's people, they found a watery grave. Miriam's brother Moses had just led the people to experience a tremendous miracle of God.

Read Exodus 15:20–21. How did Miriam respond to this miracle?

_____

_____

_____

Have you ever experienced a miracle in your own life? How did you respond?

_____

_____

_____

_____

Miriam wasn't content to keep her excitement to herself. She was a leader and role model to the women. She led them to worship God. Verse 20 refers to her as a prophetess. This meant that she received revelations from God. She was intimate with Him.

Do you regularly hear from God through time spent in His Word? Circle one.
A. All the time
B. No way
C. I'm not sure
D. Other _____

Those who hear Him most know His Word best. If you want intimacy with Him you must spend time with Him reading and studying His Word.

Miriam was a strong leader. Can't you just picture all the women gathered around her praising God?

Micah 6:4 says, "I brought you up out of Egypt and redeemed you from the land of slavery. I sent Moses to lead you, also Aaron and Miriam."

God not only used Moses and his brother Aaron, he used Miriam as well. She displayed qualities of a godly leader. Let's take a look at some of those qualities.

1. Faithful in the little.

Read Matthew 25:21. Fill in the blanks with the missing words.
"You have been _____ with a _____ things; I will put you in _____ of _____ things."

Young Miriam was diligent to watch over her brother. Although this wasn't a glamorous job, she did it to the best of her ability. When we honor God in the little things, while no one is looking, He knows He can trust us with bigger assignments.

2. Lived a life of praise.

Miriam didn't gather praise for herself. Instead she focused on giving praise where it was due. What about you? Do you draw attention to yourself or are you content to give praise and glory to God?

3. Led others to God.

How did Miriam lead others to follow God? Circle one.
A. Preaching
B. Following Him and setting an example
C. Putting up posters
D. Protesting

When people followed Miriam she taught them to follow God. When people pattern their lives after you, are they challenged to follow God? Explain your answer.

_____

_____

_____

Good leaders don't need the best personalities or the most friends. They simply must be good followers—of Jesus Christ. Do you want to be a role model today? Then follow as closely as you can in the footsteps of Jesus Christ.

Day 3: Diagnosis—Big Mouth Disease

Most of us have trouble with our big mouths, don't we? Even though Miriam was a leader, she was just like the rest of us. She had to keep her mouth in check or it would run away. Let's read about what happened in Numbers 12:1–9.

Has there ever been a time when you regretted something you said? Maybe it was to a friend or family member. Maybe it was behind their backs. What were the results?

_____

_____

_____

_____

_____

_____

Read James 3:2. Fill in the blanks with the missing words.
"We _____ stumble in many ways. If anyone is never at fault in what he _____ , he is a _____ man, able to keep his _____body in check."

How did Miriam and her brother Aaron sin with their tongues? Circle one.
   A. **Lying**
   B. **Criticizing**
   C. **Cursing**
   D. **Other** _____

They criticized Moses and his wife. They were probably struggling with envy. They saw how the people followed and respected Moses and wished it could have been them instead. Envy sneaks up on us when we don't even recognize it.

When was the last time you were envious of another person because of something they had or something they were? How did you respond?

_____

_____

_____

_____

As soon as these feelings started they should have gone straight to God in prayer. Instead they ignored God and did what came naturally. They talked about Moses and his wife behind their backs.

You may be thinking that this was pretty minor in comparison to what they could have done. Today people kill others because of envy. They steal their property. What can a few words do? After all, "Sticks and stones can break my bones, but words can never hurt me." Let's see what God says about that.

Read James 3:6–10. What do these passages warn us about our tongues?

_____

_____

_____

There are a few areas where girls especially need to be careful with their words.

1. Gossip—You knew it was coming, didn't you? It should be an Olympic sport for some girls; they're so good at it. Maybe that's you. Gossip is saying about someone what you would not say about him or her if they were present. Ouch!

Do you need to watch your mouth when it comes to gossip? Circle one.
A. No way!
B. Yes
C. Sometimes
D. Other _____

2. Lying—Sometimes it's easier to lie than tell the truth, isn't it? But it's also deadly. One lie will never be enough. When the enemy gets you in the habit of lying, he is tightening a noose around your neck. Are you committed to telling the truth even when it hurts?

3. Harsh words—This is the hardest to guard in our families. Do you speak respectfully to your parents? Are you careful about the way you talk to your brothers and sisters? A girl I know still regrets the way she talked to her younger brother growing up. Even though she's apologized, their relationship is distant.

Matthew 12:36 says, "But I tell you that men will have to give account on the day of judgment for every careless word they have spoken."

Wow! That makes you stop and think, doesn't it?

Before we close, look one more time at Numbers 12:2—"And the Lord heard this."

God called Miriam and Aaron before Him and reprimanded them. Verse 9 says that when He was finished, "The anger of the Lord burned against them, and he left them."

In your own conversations, are you aware of the fact that God is listening? Will you make it a point to honor Him in every word you speak? Good leaders are very careful with their words.

Day 4: Costly Words

Read Numbers 12:1–15. Ask God to teach you from His Word today.

Yesterday we studied Miriam and Aaron's sin of the tongue. Today we'll look at another way they disobeyed God. Hopefully we can learn to avoid their mistakes.

Have your parents ever called you and your brothers and sisters to speak to them, and you knew by your parents' tone of voice it wasn't going to be pretty? That must have been how Miriam and Aaron felt when God called them before Himself.

Summarize what God told them in verses 6–8.

_____

_____

_____

Why was it a sin that they spoke out against Moses? Circle one.
A. **He got his feelings hurt easily**
B. **He was God's chosen leader**
C. **He had a bad temper**
D. **Other** _____

Moses was chosen by God to lead His people out of Egypt to the land He promised them. When they spoke against the authority God placed over them, they spoke against God Himself. This is dangerous business. We must be cautious about speaking against those God has placed over us.

Read Romans 13:1–2. Fill in the blanks with the missing words.
"_____ must submit himself to the governing _____, for there is no authority except that which God has established. The authorities that _____ have been _____ by God. Consequently, he who _____ against the authority is rebelling against what God has _____ , and those who do so will bring _____ on themselves."

What happens to those who rebel against the authority God has placed over them?

_____

_____

_____

What happened to Miriam because she spoke out against Moses?

_____

_____

_____

Just as Miriam publicly spoke out against her brother, she was publicly disgraced. Miriam was struck with leprosy, a most dreaded disease, and sent out from the camp for a week. Not only was she miserable, but the rest of the people had to wait a week before they could move forward on their journey to the Promised Land. Her sin not only affected her, it impacted the rest of her people.

What authorities has God placed over your life? List those in your home, school, and in our country.

Do you find it easy to obey those God has placed over you? Circle one.

A. No way!

B. Yes, I do it for my own good

C. Sometimes

D. Other _____

Have you ever considered that when you disobey your parents and teachers you are really disobeying God? If you struggle with learning this lesson you may want to write the following verse in a place where you'll see it often. It's better to learn the lesson of authority than suffer the consequences as Miriam did. As a leader, you will be accountable to God and others in authority over you.

> *"Obey your leaders and submit to their authority. They keep watch over you as men who must give an account. Obey them so that their work will be a joy, not a burden, for that would be of no advantage to you."* —HEBREWS 13:17

Day 5: Moving On

Maybe as we've studied Miriam this week you've seen a lot of yourself in her personality. Just like all of us, she had strengths and weaknesses.

List some of those below.

Strengths:

_____

_____

_____

_____

_____

_____

_____

Weaknesses:

_____

_____

_____

_____

_____

_____

_____

Miriam definitely had a strong personality. She was probably one of those people that others noticed. At her best she led others to follow God, while at her worst she was critical and backbiting.

While God loves us just as we are, He disciplines us when we choose sin. His discipline is designed to teach us to turn away from sin. He allows consequences to come into our lives to reinforce godly decisions.

Can you recall a time when you experienced consequences for a sinful choice you made? What were they?

_____

_____

_____

_____

Reread Numbers 12:9–15. Isn't it easier to recognize what we've done wrong after we've done it?

In verse 11 Aaron realizes what sin they have committed. What does he ask of Moses?

_____

_____

_____

It's harder to recognize sinful words or actions before they happen, but the more we guard our minds the easier it will be to stop sinful actions in their tracks. Miriam and Aaron should have thought more carefully before they spoke.

How do you think Miriam felt when the Lord was disciplining her?

_____

_____

_____

_____

Do you think the consequences helped her learn her lesson? Circle one.

A. Definitely

B. No way!

C. Maybe

D. Other _____

Have your parents ever sent you to your room to "think about what you did"? Miriam's banishment from the camp sounds a little bit like that, doesn't it? She had a whole week to think about what she did—and how she wouldn't do it again. You can bet the next time she was tempted to open that mouth in criticism, she seriously considered the consequences.

Oh, the mercy of God! Where would we be without it? The very last words in verse 15 say "she was brought back." God lovingly disciplines us to teach us, and then by His grace He brings us back. We can come to Him in repentance because He willingly forgives us.

Read Psalm 86:5. Fill in the blanks with the missing words.

"You are _____ and good, O Lord, abounding in _____ to all who _____ to you."

God forgave Miriam and brought her back into the camp. He does the same with us when we sin. How do you think Miriam felt after she returned to the camp? She was probably blown away by God's grace. She was probably changed—for the better.

After you've repented from sin, has it changed the way you acted? Circle one.

A. No

B. Yes

C. I'm not sure

D. Other _____

Now read Numbers 20:1. We come to the end of Miriam's life. The fact that a woman's death was even recorded in those days shows her great honor.

Aren't you glad the Bible tells the whole truth about people? It challenges us to become more Christlike and to avoid the mistakes they made.

Action Point ● ● ● ● ● ● ● ● ● ● ● ● ● ● ● ●

At the top of a piece of paper write out Romans 13:1–2. Under those verses make a list of the authorities God has placed in your own life. List every person you can think of, from each teacher to your youth minister. Include your parents and, if you have them, your stepparents.

After you've completed your list, prayerfully read over each name. If you've disrespected that person in the past make it a point to repent before God of that sin. Then sometime this week go to him or her and ask for their forgiveness.

Remember, when we rebel against our earthly authorities, God's Word says we're really rebelling against Him.

Week 10

Developing Your Prayer Life

Hannah

1 Samuel 1:1–2:11

Memory Verse

Philippians 4:6

"Do not be anxious about anything, but in every-thing, by prayer and petition, with thanksgiving, present your requests to God."

Memory Verse:

"Do not be anxious about anything, but in everything, by prayer and petition, with thanksgiving, present your requests to God."

—PHILIPPIANS 4:6

Julia's Story

As Julia opened the letter her heart pounded with excitement. It was from the college she had always wanted to attend. Was she accepted? She pulled out the letter and quickly realized she was accepted. She jumped up and down because her prayers were answered. In the fall she would attend the college of her dreams.

In July, before she left for school, her mother was diagnosed with cancer. Julia's feelings of excitement quickly faded. Instead she felt like her world was falling apart around her. She was torn about what to do in the fall. Should she go off to college? After all, it was her dream. Or should she stay back to help care for her mother?

After much prayer she decided that God wanted her to surrender her college plans to Him and serve her family. She called the college admissions office and told them of her change of plans. She got a job at a local bookstore to help out with hospital bills and spent the rest of her time taking care of housework and caring for her mother. Her friends who had left for college thought she was crazy. They couldn't understand her selfless decision.

About the time her friends came home for the summer she realized her mother wasn't going to live long. That summer she watched her mother die and spent almost every waking moment beside her. Looking back, Julia had no regrets for the choice she made. While she had laid down her biggest desire, she had gained something far greater. She had precious memories and the knowledge that she had served God even when the choice wasn't easy. Through her prayer and time spent with God, she knew what decision she needed to make.

Day 1: A Breaking Heart

This week we'll study a woman of prayer. This could perhaps be the most important chapter of this study. Why? Prayer changes things. More importantly, prayer changes us.

Begin your study of Hannah by reading 1 Samuel 1:1–20.

Why was Hannah upset? Circle one.
A. She had no children
B. She was sick
C. Her husband had another wife
D. Other _____

According to verse 7, Hannah was so upset she wouldn't eat. Have you ever been so sad about something that you wouldn't eat? If so, describe the situation.

_____

_____

_____

Hannah desperately wanted a child. She had been unable to get pregnant while her husband's other wife, Peninnah, had children. To make matters worse, Peninnah mocked her because of her childless condition.

Have you ever been ridiculed because of something you couldn't control? How did it make you feel?

_____

_____

_____

While God's intention for marriage was for a man to have one wife, having more than one was culturally acceptable in those days. But as shown by Hannah's story, it caused serious family problems.

Hannah was overwhelmed by sadness. What do you do when you feel like that? Circle one.

A. Get depressed

B. Talk to my girlfriends

C. Isolate myself

D. Other _____

Hannah responded the best way possible. She took her problem to God in prayer. She must have been so intent on praying that she forgot about anyone else around her. Eli, the priest, misunderstood what she was doing.

What did Eli accuse Hannah of doing?

_____

_____

_____

According to verses 15–16, how did Hannah respond?

_____

_____

_____

Earlier Hannah's husband had misunderstood her sadness. Now the priest didn't understand. The only one who truly knew her heart was God. It's the same way with us. God is the only one who you can be sure will understand and listen 100% of the time.

According to verse 18, how was she different after she had prayed about her problem?

_____

_____

_____

Prayer not only changes circumstances, it changes us. When you're hurting, do you tell God how you feel? While discussing problems with family and friends isn't bad, we must never forget to bring our problems before the God of the universe. He has the power to not only change the problem, but to change our attitude about the problem. Not only that, He gives us peace.

Are you dealing with a serious problem today? If so, bring it to God in prayer. He is waiting to hear from you.

> "Trust in him at all times, O people; pour out your hearts to him, for God is our refuge." —Psalm 62:8

Day 2: Ask Me

Hannah was a woman of prayer. She trusted God enough to tell Him her needs, and she saw Him answer her prayers. Today we're going to study how we can also become women of prayer.

Read Matthew 6:5–8. What does Jesus warn about praying so others will notice us?

_____

_____

_____

While we can pray anywhere, Jesus tells us to go into our rooms because sometimes prayer needs to be a private conversation between Him and us.

What promise is given in verse 8?

_____

_____

_____

Isn't that good news? He already knows what you need. Then why pray? In prayer we acknowledge our dependence on Him. The main reason we pray is because He tells us to pray.

Now read Matthew 7:7–11. In what three actions are we commanded to persevere according to verse 7?

_____

_____

_____

_____

Have you ever prayed about something and felt like God didn't answer? If so, describe the situation.

_____

_____

_____

_____

God answers every prayer His children pray. Sometimes He says "no." Why no? Well, sometimes we ask for something that isn't good for us. He knows what's best and, like the perfect Father He is, tells us no.

Have you ever received a "no" answer to a prayer? Circle one.
A. Never
B. Yes
C. No
D. Other _____

Sometimes God says "wait." This is probably the hardest answer of all. Have you ever noticed that we are people who hate to wait—in line, on the phone, and especially for something we want? But God's timing is so much better than ours. He sees the big picture and knows how He's working behind the scenes. So if you get a "wait" answer, just keep praying and trust that His plans are better than yours ever could be.

Often, God will say "yes." Can you recall a situation when you prayed about something and God answered your prayer with a yes? If so, describe what happened.

_____

_____

_____

Read John 14:14. Fill in the blanks with the missing words.
"You may _____ me for _____ in my name, and I will
_____ it."

What an amazing promise! Jesus is basically saying that if it is according to His will He will give us what we ask. How do you know whether something is according to His will or not? Does it line up with God's Word? Is it something that brings God glory?

Sometimes we may not know whether a request is in His will, but we are still welcome to ask—like Hannah did. Ask Him and believe that He is fully capable of answering your prayer. He is waiting to hear from you. Are you ready to pray?

"Jesus looked at them and said, 'With man this is impossible, but not with God; all things are possible with God.'" —MARK 10:27

Day 3: A Promise Kept

Have you ever promised something and then later realized that to fulfill your promise would cost you dearly? Maybe you made a promise to a parent, a friend, or even God. Maybe you even regretted your promise later.

I wonder if Hannah felt that way about the promise she made to God. Read 1 Samuel 1:10–28.

According to verse 10, what did Hannah promise God if He gave her a son? Circle one.
A. To serve God
B. To give him back to God
C. To pray more
D. To get a haircut

Did Hannah keep her promise? If so, how do you think she felt?

_____

_____

_____

When Samuel was approximately three years old, Hannah took him to live with Eli the priest, where he would prepare to one day also become a priest. Samuel's tasks as a young boy probably included caring for and cleaning the Tabernacle. As he grew older, he probably helped with the sacrifices.

Read 1 Samuel 1:27–28. Fill in the blanks with Hannah's words.
"I _____ for this child, and the _____ has granted me what I _____ of him. So now I _____ him to the LORD. For his _____ life he will be _____ over to the LORD."

Hannah gave up what she had asked for in order to keep her promise to God. Could you have done the same thing? Why or why not?

_____

_____

_____

Hannah realized that Samuel's life was a gift from God. He wasn't hers anyway, so she was just returning to God what He had given her. She gave God what was most precious to her.

When you give to God, do you give gifts that mean nothing to you or are you willing to give sacrificially? Circle one.
A. I give sacrificially
B. I don't give anything
C. I give what's easy to give
D. Other _____

James 1:17 says, "Every good and perfect gift is from above, coming down from the Father of the heavenly lights, who does not change like shifting shadows."

Do you recognize that the gifts in your life are ultimately from your heavenly Father? Has God given you a gift you've kept for yourself? Are you willing to give it back to Him? Explain your answer.

_____

_____

_____

Maybe He answered your prayer to be in a certain club at school or have a date with a Christian guy. Are you willing to honor God in the way you handle those gifts?

Ecclesiastes 5:4–5 says, "When you make a vow to God, do not delay in fulfilling it. He has no pleasure in fools; fulfill your vow. It is better not to vow than to make a vow and not fulfill it."

Do you keep your word, to God and others, even when it may hurt? Explain your answer.

_____

_____

_____

Because of Hannah's devotion to God and her willingness to follow through with her word, Samuel grew up to become one of the greatest prophets and priests in Israel's history. He led many to follow God. Hannah's actions made not only a difference on her son, but on a whole nation.

Day 4: Remember Who God Is

Imagine that you give someone a wonderful gift. They are so excited that they forget to thank you and run off to enjoy their new treasure. How would you feel?

How do you respond when God answers your prayers? Do you thank Him for His answers? Or do you forget you even prayed in the first place?

_____

_____

_____

It's so easy to forget about God when we get what we want, isn't it? Sometimes it's easier to follow God when we're "needy." Today we'll study how Hannah responded to God's gift of Samuel, her son.

Read 1 Samuel 2:1–11. If you summed up the passage in one phrase, what would it be? Circle one.
A. God is in control of everything
B. God doesn't care about us
C. Hannah loves Samuel
D. Other _____

Hannah recognized that while God runs the entire universe—knowing each detail of every person, plant, and animal—He also cares for the needs of one sorrowful woman. While God sees every person in the world, He intimately knows our hearts. He knows what makes you happy, excited, and sad. Not only does He know—He cares deeply for you. That's the beauty of prayer. We don't come to an impersonal God asking something, we come to our Heavenly Father.

Maybe you have the kind of dad who isn't safe to approach—or maybe you have one who is always ready to hear from you. Picture the kind of father whose lap you can crawl into and tell him what you need. This is your Heavenly Father. He waits to hear from you.

Read Isaiah 30:18. Fill in the blanks with the missing words.
"Yet the LORD _____ to be _____ to you; he _____ to show you _____ . For the LORD is a God of _____ . Blessed are all who _____ for _____!"

Hannah realized that prayer is more about God than it is about us. She didn't simply see God as a big vending machine in the sky—put in your request and out pops an answer. No, she approached God for who He is, holy and mighty.

When you pray, do you remember to worship God for who He is? Circle one.

A. No

B. Yes

C. Sometimes

D. Other _____

Sometimes in prayer we become too focused on receiving the answer, when our main focus should be on God. He is enough, no matter what answer He gives us, whether it's no, wait, or yes.

Hannah was able to give Samuel back to God because she knew God made her life complete—not Samuel.

Have you learned the same lesson about prayer? Explain your answer.

_____

_____

_____

The next time you begin praying, don't just start listing your requests to God. Take some time to acknowledge who He is. You may want to use Hannah's prayer in 1 Samuel 2:1–11 as a guide. This passage describes God's character and actions. It will remind you of just how *huge* God is. Check your heart to see if you have sin you need to confess to Him. Make sure you come before Him in purity and honesty. He is waiting to hear from you.

Day 5: Power Unleashed

Do you want God to use you in this world? Do you desire to take part in His worldwide plan to bring people to know Him? Do you want to see

His will accomplished on the earth? Do you want to see change—in circumstances and people? If you answered yes to any of these questions, then you desire to become a woman of prayer. Prayer is the one thing that unleashes God's power in your world.

Do you want to become a woman of prayer? Circle one.
A. Yes
B. Maybe
C. No
D. Other _____

I grew up knowing I should pray, but not always knowing how to go about it. Maybe you can relate. Today we're going to look at some practical ways to develop a stronger prayer life.

What is the biggest obstacle you face in deepening your prayer life? It could be that you have a short attention span or a busy schedule. List the obstacle in the space provided.

_____

What can you do to help you overcome this obstacle?

_____
_____
_____

Maybe when you start to pray your mind immediately wanders. How can you stay focused? One way is by writing out your prayers. We've used this method in our study a few times. You might want to find a special notebook where you write your prayers like letters to God. One benefit of this method is you always have your prayers recorded. You can see how God answered!

It's a good idea to at least list requests so you don't forget them. How many times have you told someone you would pray for them and then forgotten all about it? If you're like me, that's happened too many times.

Another way to keep your mind from wandering is to pray aloud when you're alone. You can pray aloud in the shower, when you're taking a walk, or—if you have your driver's license—while you drive. This is a great reminder that God is with you all the time.

Read 1 Thessalonians 5:16–18. How often should we pray? Circle one.
A. When we remember
B. Often
C. Continually
D. At meals

This doesn't mean we drop out of school and all activities in order to pray all the time. Instead, we're to go about our days with a constant attitude of prayer. When you see someone who needs Jesus you can pray right then. When you need guidance, ask God immediately. We are to live with our spiritual "channel" constantly tuned into talking to Jesus.

Another way to strengthen your prayer muscles is to get a prayer partner. You may want to ask a friend or even an older lady you know who has a strong prayer life. Prayer partners don't take the place of private prayer, but they do help build consistency. You and your partner could meet weekly to pray, or you could even pray over the phone. Make sure you do more praying than talking and that you guard against gossip.

Read James 5:13–18. According to verse 16, the prayer of a righteous person is what?

If you are a Christian, God's Word says you are righteous. Prayer isn't so much about who prays, but *Whom* you are asking. You are asking the all-powerful God of the universe. Nothing is too difficult for Him.

Read Jeremiah 29:12. What promise is given?

Wow! God is waiting to hear from you. As we end this week, use the space provided to write a prayer to God. Ask Him to deepen your prayer life and help you to know Him more. Commit to set aside time each day to bring your prayers to Him. Remember, the Christian life is a relationship. Will you devote time to nurture your relationship with Jesus?

_____

_____

_____

_____

_____

_____

_____

_____

_____

Action Point

Have you ever sat down to pray and been overwhelmed by all of the needs there were to pray for? Prayer doesn't have to be that way. Remember that prayer is a simple conversation between the heavenly Father and His loved child.

On a sheet of paper list all of the things you want to pray about. You may want to include your family needs, school life, decisions you'll be making, lost friends, church leaders, and our nation. Now take a separate sheet of paper and make columns with the different days of the week. Under each day write down different prayer reminders. You may also want to make a separate column that says "Every day" where you include things to pray for daily. Refer to this list when you pray. While this system may not work for everyone, it just may help you become more consistent in your prayer life. Try it for a week and see.

Week 11

Discovering Your Gifts

Phoebe

Romans 16:1–2

Memory Verse

Jeremiah 29:11

" 'For I know the plans I have for you,' declares the Lord, 'plans to prosper you and not to harm you, plans to give you hope and a future.' "

Memory Verse:

" 'For I know the plans I have for you,' declares the Lord, 'plans to prosper you and not to harm you, plans to give you hope and a future.' "

— Jeremiah 29:11

Becky's Story

All of her life Becky's family had struggled financially. They never had enough money for her to be a girl scout when she was younger, and the older she got the situation seemed to worsen. She always turned down offers to school dances because she knew it would be a hardship on her family to buy a dress. She determined that no matter what happened in her future she would one day be rich. That was her very first priority.

She received a college scholarship to a very competitive school and began her first year in the pre-law program. She was going to be a lawyer. Nothing could stop her until one morning when she was praying during her quiet time. She started to feel God calling her to lay down her plans before Him and to pray about what He wanted to do with her life. So she immediately focused her thoughts on God.

After this happened for several mornings, she just couldn't ignore that God was trying to get her attention. She began asking Him each morning what career path He wanted her to pursue. At the end of several months she decided to change her major from pre-law to ministry. She felt God steering her down this new path, one that better used the gifts God had given her. Although she knew she would never be rich, with this decision she knew that God was honored. It wasn't that she couldn't serve God and be a lawyer, but rather that He had a unique plan for her that He was waiting to unfold.

Today she serves in a ministry to troubled teenage girls. She may not have new clothes every season, but she has the unmistakable peace that comes when we surrender our lives to the plans of God. She discovered wonderful gifts that God had given her, like a compassionate heart and mercy toward others. Now she uses those gifts for God's glory.

Day 1: Not Your Typical Friend

This week we're going to study a little-known woman in the early church. You might not have heard of Phoebe, but she is an excellent role model for Christian young women today. Let's get started. Read Romans 16:1–2.

List what you discovered about Phoebe from these verses.

_____

_____

_____

_____

_____

Phoebe was probably a wealthy woman who may have supported Paul's ministry financially. She lived in the little town of Cenchrea that was the eastern seaport of Corinth, a bustling big city in that time. In the verses you read, Paul spoke very highly of Phoebe. She, like Priscilla, must have made a big difference in the life of the early church.

God wants to use women today just as He did back then. Each of us is uniquely gifted for service in His kingdom. Throughout history God used all kinds of women to do all kinds of jobs. He is looking for women today who are available to Him. Are you one of those young women? This week we'll study characteristics of the women He uses by studying the life of Phoebe.

How does Paul tell the readers of the Roman letter to treat Phoebe? Circle one.
A. **Like an outsider**
B. **In a way worthy of a saint**
C. **Kindly**
D. **Other** _____

Wow! This tells us a lot about Phoebe. Phoebe must have proven that she was worthy of being treated like a saint, if Paul told them to treat her that way. *Saint* was a word Paul used to refer to fellow believers.

Would someone be able to say that you are worthy of being treated as a saint, based on your behavior? Circle one.

A. Possibly

B. No way

C. Who, me?

D. Yes

She must have lived her life in such a way that others noticed her purity and devotion to the Lord.

Do you know anyone who lives like that? What is she like?

_____

_____

_____

Read Ephesians 5:1–4. According to these verses, describe how Christians are to live.

_____

_____

_____

Is there an area where you need to allow God to change you so you can walk in obedience to His commands? If so, let Him change you today!

Ephesians 5:1 tells us to be imitators of God because we are dearly loved children of God. What better reason is there for walking in purity before Him? If you are a Christian today you are dearly loved and wonderfully prized. Will you behave like the lavishly loved child that you are? Phoebe did—and so can you.

Day 2: Whose Feet Can I Wash?

Today we'll continue to look at some characteristics of women God uses. Reread Romans 16:1–2.

What word does Paul use in verse 1 to describe Phoebe? Circle one.
A. Prayer warrior
B. Loudmouth
C. Servant
D. Missionary

The word Paul wrote literally means "deaconess." Did you know that whatever task deacons or deaconesses carry out, they are supposed to be servants? Whether they take up the offering, visit sick people, or help with the parking, they should model servanthood. Phoebe must have served devotedly if Paul referred to her as deaconess.

Do you know anyone who is a true servant? If so, describe their actions.

_____

_____

_____

Servants model the behavior of their Lord. Jesus was the greatest picture of a servant that the world has ever seen. Read John 13:1–17.

What act of servanthood did Jesus perform in this passage?

_____

_____

_____

What command did He give His disciples in verses 14–15?

_____

_____

_____

Although we may not literally wash our friends' feet, there are things we can do to serve them. How can you wash others' feet? There may be someone in your family who needs help or encouragement. Maybe you need to humble yourself and forgive a friend. There are always opportunities to serve. The challenge is being aware of them and then acting on them.

Last week we studied about serving in our churches. Maybe you could dedicate one Sunday a month to help with the babies or children. Or you could visit the elderly in a nursing home. What can you do as a young woman to serve God?

Phoebe didn't have to be in the limelight. What do I mean by that? Well, true servants don't need their actions broadcast. They don't serve to get credit. Often they serve behind the scenes and let God be their only audience.

What about you? When you do something to serve another person, do you seek credit and attention or are you content to let it be a secret between you and God? Circle one.

A. I love for people to notice me

B. I keep it a secret

C. I haven't thought about it

D. Other _____

Phoebe may have served by giving financially to the ministry of the church. God calls each Christian to give a tithe, or tenth, of his or her income to His church. Many give an offering of even more than that.

Malachi 3:10 says, "-'Bring the whole tithe into the storehouse, that there may be food in my house. Test me in this,' says the LORD Almighty, 'and see if I will not throw open the floodgates of heaven and pour out so much blessing that you will not have room enough for it.'"

We are not only commanded to tithe, but God blesses us when we tithe. Do you earn money from a job or from chores around the house? Maybe you receive an allowance.

Will you commit to give God ten percent, or a tithe, of that? Why or why not?

_____

_____

_____

A true test of whether or not we trust God is how we use our money and resources. Our money reveals whom we truly serve, God or ourselves. Are you committed to serving God wholeheartedly, in every area of your life?

Day 3: Worthy Life?

This week we're studying characteristics of Phoebe and discovering our own unique gifts for reaching the world for Jesus. He's seeking those who live in constant availability to His plans and are willing to use what He has given them. They surrender their resources, talents, and spiritual gifts to His service. But mostly, they make themselves available to do whatever He asks.

Have you ever looked at someone else and thought that they had more to "offer" God than you? Maybe she was more talented, prettier, more popular, or had more knowledge. Circle one.

A. Yes

B. Never

C. Every now and then

D. Other _____

Read 1 Corinthians 1:26–31. This passage teaches that God often chooses to use weak things and weak people.

According to verse 29, why does He do this?

_____

_____

_____

_____

We should never boast in our own talents and potential, because on our own we're nothing. It's only when we're yielded to Christ that He uses us for His purposes and glory. When we empty ourselves of pride, we can then be filled with Him.

While there's nothing wrong with confidence, our confidence needs to be in God rather than ourselves. Which kind of confidence do you rely on most? Circle one.

A. Confidence in self

B. Confidence in God

C. Neither

D. Other _____

Reread 1 Corinthians 1:31. Fill in the blanks with the missing words.
"Let him who _____ boast in the _____ ."

Just as God used Phoebe in the first century, God wants to use you too. He has unique plans for your life. He wants to do something through you that He won't do through your sister, friend, or pastor. The key isn't how talented you are, it's how yielded you are to Him. God is forming you into a godly young woman to be used in His service.

Now read Ephesians 4:1. What are we called to do in this verse?

_____

_____

_____

"A life worthy." It doesn't mean we're perfect, but that we strive for obedience and purity in our daily lives. Does this describe you? Explain your answer.

_____

_____

_____

Have you ever wondered what God's plans were for your life? What job does He want you to take? What man will you marry someday? Where will you live? Maybe you, like me, have tried to get Him to tell you the plans. Maybe you've looked in the Bible to see if there's anything specific for you. While He doesn't often tell us what's ahead, we can trust Him.

Obedience, day by day, will get you where you need to be in the future.

Do you purpose to live in obedience and purity before Him? Are there areas in your life where you need to give over control to Him? If so, spend some time praying about those areas as we end today. Surrender to Him so you will live a life worthy of His calling.

Day 4: Carry It with You

God uses all kinds of people for all kinds of missions. He uses women and men, young and old, educated and uneducated. As we saw yesterday, He isn't looking at our qualifications as much as our availability.

Let's look at another characteristic of those God uses. Reread Romans 16:1–2. One way Phoebe was thought to have helped Paul was by carrying his letters. Research suggests that she may have even carried this letter from Paul to Rome from Corinth. She was trustworthy. She knew how to handle the words of Paul. She handled carefully the Book of Romans, a very important part of the Word of God.

Read 2 Timothy 2:15. Fill in the blanks with the missing words.
"Do your _____ to present yourself to _____ as one approved, a _____ who does not need to be ashamed and who _____ handles the _____ of _____."

Do you handle the Word of God with care? I am not asking you how clean and tidy your Bible is. Some have said that those with Bibles that look like they are falling apart from use represent lives that aren't falling apart. Do you study and learn from the Bible? Do you memorize it? Is it a top priority for you?

Read James 1:22–25. What does this passage teach we must do to be blessed by God? Circle one.
A. Memorize the Bible
B. Act out Bible stories
C. Do what the Bible says
D. Pray constantly

God uses those who know and obey His Word. The more you study the Bible, the more you know the Author. That's just the way it is.

Are you willing to set aside time daily for Bible reading and study? Explain your answer.

_____

I'm so proud of you for sticking with this Bible study for all these weeks. I know it's a commitment and that you have a lot going on. I trust that as you've studied, you've seen how God's Word relates to all issues of life. It teaches and guides us. It comforts us. It helps us know God more. It changes us from the inside out.

In what ways have you changed as a result of your time spent studying the Bible?

_____

_____

_____

When this study ends in a couple of weeks, don't stop reading your Bible. Don't stop memorizing Bible verses. You may want to ask some friends to start a new study with you. Or you may find another study to do alone. Whatever you do, keep your commitment to study the Word of God.

You may want to find longer passages to memorize. Some people commit chapters or short Bible books to memory. While it sounds difficult, it's very possible. Just think of all the song lyrics you have rolling around in your brain.

Now read Joshua 1:8. What promise is given for those who live their lives with a high commitment to the Word of God?

_____

_____

_____

_____

Are you willing to keep the daily habit of studying His Word? Circle one.

A. I'll think about it

B. Yes

C. No

D. Other _____

Will you, like Phoebe, carry the Word of God with you wherever you go? Will you hide it in your heart and live according to what it says? If so, He will use you mightily on this earth.

> *"I have hidden your word in my heart that I might not sin against you."* —PSALM 119:11

Day 5: You're a Minister

God wants to use you in this world. He will use you as you live each day in obedience and faith before Him. He has uniquely gifted you in order to use your life. You are 100% handcrafted and designed by your Creator for a special purpose on this planet.

Are you willing to let Him work through you to touch your world? Do you remember how Paul described Phoebe as one who helped many people? Who can you help today? Will you step out of your comfort zone and serve someone? We can tell people all day long about Jesus' love, but until we show it to them they won't fully understand.

Read Romans 12:4–8. This passage discusses spiritual gifts. Spiritual gifts are given to believers by the Holy Spirit in order to be used for ministry. Each Christian has at least one, while many may have more.

List some of the spiritual gifts that this passage discusses.

_____

_____

_____

_____

You may or may not know what your spiritual gifts are. One way to find out is by asking those close to you. They may have some idea as they've seen you exercise your gifts in ministry. You can pray that God will show you your gifts. There are wonderful tests and inventories your church probably has that will help you discover what spiritual gifts you have. Finding out your gifts helps you find ministry opportunities that match the way you are gifted.

Have you ever found out what your spiritual gifts are? Circle one.
A. I've never even heard of them.
B. No
C. Yes
D. Other _____

No one gift is more important than another gift. While some may be more visible, they are all essential in helping the body of Christ to function as a healthy whole.

Read 1 Corinthians 12:14–20. According to verse 18, who distributes the spiritual gifts?
_____
_____

When we know our spiritual gifts, it's important that we don't focus too much on those, but on God. The more we know Him, the more He'll use us. Why do you think this is?
_____
_____
_____

You are a minister. God wants to use you to minister to this hurting and lost world. When you look in the mirror each morning, remind yourself that you see a minister of God looking back. Your youth minister doesn't go to your school—but you do. Your pastor could never make the cheerleading squad—but you might. Your Bible study teacher couldn't play in the band—but God may have put you there. He has strategically placed you in order to use you.

Will you let Him? Circle one.
A. Who, me?
B. Maybe
C. Yes
D. Other _____

Read Matthew 5:14–16. In what way can you let your light shine before a dark world this week?

_____

_____

_____

When we see our lives fit into the greater purposes of God in this world, we start to find fulfillment like we've never had before. God has plans for you—amazing and wonderful plans. Are you willing to discover your gifts and use them for God's glory?

Action Point

This week we're going to put our servant's robes on. Remember that we said servants don't serve in order to receive credit. Instead, they help others so God will get the glory.

Do you like secrets? Well, this week's action point is a secret between you and God. Start off by asking God how He wants you to serve someone this week. When you hear from Him, don't tell anyone your plan. Next, carry out your act of service without telling anyone. You may clean up a part of your house, write an anonymous note encouraging someone, or give a small gift or even cash to someone in need. Remember, the key is to help someone with a need without them knowing who did it. You may want to leave a note that says something like, "I just wanted to brighten your day in the name of Jesus. Love, His servant" Be as creative as you'd like to be and try to use your unique gifts. When you get together with your group, resist the urge to tell them what you did. Let this forever be your secret between you and God.

Week 12

Reaching the World

Priscilla

Acts 18:1–3, 18, 24–26;
Romans 16:3–4; 1 Corinthians 16:19

Memory Verse

Philippians 2:5

"Your attitude should be the same as that of Christ Jesus."

Memory Verse:

"Your attitude should be the same as that of Christ Jesus."

—PHILIPPIANS 2:5

Anne's Story

Life had never been better. Anne was dating a wonderful guy, had an incredible summer job, and couldn't wait to start her second year of college. She was home for the summer and became active in the college ministry at her church. She joined a Bible study where she learned to apply Scripture to everyday life.

One Tuesday night at Bible study a missionary from India spoke. She was a petite young woman who told about her life in the city of Calcutta. Anne hung onto her every word. The pictures of the Indian children pulled on her heart. After the meeting the missionary told Anne more stories about her missionary life. Anne went home that night with a growing compassion for the lost of India.

Over the next few weeks, Anne seemed to constantly think about the people in India who did not know Jesus. Each time she read the Bible, the missions call grew louder. She began to pray about whether God wanted her to go to the mission field. Questions raced through her mind such as, "Will I ever get married?" and "Will I be safe?" But in spite of her questions, she knew God was setting her life apart for something she could only dream of.

She committed her life to missions and left the rest up to Him. She trusted God with whether or not she would marry. She trusted Him with her health and everything concerning her future. If you asked her today she would say that surrendering your whole life to God is the best way to live. Anything less isn't really living.

Day 1: Strong When Persecuted

Have you ever wondered what it would have been like to be a Christian back in biblical times? Those must have been exciting days, seeing God work as the number of followers of Jesus grew. They were also scary days. Persecution of Christians was brutal. To follow Jesus meant risking one's life.

This week we'll meet Priscilla. The Bible doesn't tell us a lot about her, but we know she helped shape the early church by her life and ministry. She is mentioned as a coworker with the apostle Paul. Let's see what we can find out about this radical follower of Jesus and how she reached her world for Christ. Read Acts 18:1–3.

Why were Priscilla and her husband Aquila in Corinth?

_____

_____

_____

Have you ever been excluded or persecuted because of your faith? If so, describe the situation.

_____

_____

_____

Aquila and Priscilla were forced to leave their home because of their faith. This is hard to understand for people like us who enjoy religious freedom.

How do you think they felt when forced to start over in a new place?

_____

_____

_____

Today in many parts of the world people are martyred for their faith in Christ. Some religions demand that families disown or even murder those who convert to Christianity. For some, making a commitment to Jesus Christ may cost them everything—even their own lives.

Have you ever suffered a loss because you followed Jesus? Circle one.

A. No way

B. Yes

C. Minor losses

D. Other_____

Read 2 Timothy 3:12. What does this passage teach about persecution? Circle one.

A. It won't happen if we obey God

B. We can expect it

C. It only happens to missionaries

D. Other _____

Maybe your family hasn't disowned you because of your faith, but do they mock your decision? Do people at school laugh at you for your convictions? Persecution can either make us stronger in our faith or make us weaker. When we rely on Christ's strength we're able to stand up in spite of persecution, but when we depend on ourselves we'll fall in defeat.

Priscilla and Aquila relied on God and He used them to impact the early church. Today we are living legacies of the seeds they planted.

As we end today, write a prayer asking God to help you boldly stand up for Him. He will strengthen you as you rely on Him.

_____

_____

_____

_____

_____

_____

_____

_____

_____

_____

_____

Day 2: Hand in Hand

Priscilla was definitely a woman who was ahead of her time. God used her to radically shape the early church and set the stage for today's church. Read 1 Corinthians 16:19 and Romans 16:3–4.

What did they risk for the sake of Paul and the gospel of Christ? Circle one.
A. Their home
B. Their reputations
C. Their lives
D. Their sanity

We don't know what kind of a risk they took, but we do know it must have been something big if Paul mentioned it in his letter to the Romans.

Have you ever risked something valuable for the cause of Jesus? If so, describe the situation.

_____

_____

_____

_____

Priscilla and Aquila must have had a radical marriage. They weren't content to just settle into life and acquire a lot of stuff. Their goals were much different. They sought to further the name of Jesus no matter what it cost them.

Do you know any couples who have those same goals? If so, describe their marriage.

_____

_____

_____

_____

I am reminded of the prayer my husband prayed at our own wedding. As we knelt before God he didn't pray for wealth, health, or blessings. Instead, he asked God to use our marriage for His purposes on the earth—no matter what.

Every time Priscilla or Aquila is mentioned in the Bible, the other is mentioned as well. They were partners in more than just marriage—they were ministry partners too. They taught others, they opened their home for other Christians, and when they returned to Rome they began one of the house churches there. They had the same heart for the Lord.

When you think about your own marriage someday, do you picture yourself like this couple? Do you want to serve God together? If so, remember that the guys you spend time with today will help determine what kind of man you marry.

Do you make wise choices regarding guy friends and dates? Circle one.
A. Sometimes
B. Yes, I follow God's standards
C. No
D. Other _____

Read 2 Corinthians 6:14–16. What does this passage teach about being joined with unbelievers?

_____

_____

_____

_____

God wants all of your relationships to glorify Him. Do your friendships with guys draw you closer to Christ? What about the guys you date? Does being with that someone special increase your desire to follow God and walk in His ways? If so, this is a relationship that can honor God. If not, it will lead you to compromise and heartache. Will you make the necessary changes?

When evaluating guy friends and potential dates, consider whether you can picture yourself serving God together. I know a couple that found places to serve together for many of their dates. They took food to the needy, volunteered in retirement homes, and helped out at their church. Their relationship was built on a solid foundation. Today they have a wonderful marriage and serve together on a ministry staff. They are a modern-day Priscilla and Aquila.

Read Romans 15:5–6. Fill in the blanks with the missing words.
"May the God who gives _____ and
_____ give you a spirit of _____
among yourselves as you follow _____ _____ , so
that with one _____ and _____ you may
_____ the God and Father of our Lord Jesus Christ."

Does this verse describe the kind of relationships you strive after? If not, will you make changes so that it will?

Day 3: Pass It On

Priscilla was a servant. Everywhere her name is mentioned in Scripture you find her helping and ministering. Today we're going to study how she specifically ministered to her fellow Christians.

Read Romans 16:3–4. How did the churches feel about Priscilla and Aquila?

_____

_____

_____

_____

They must have helped the churches in tremendous ways. Take a moment to think about your church. Would the people there say they are grateful for you? Do you help out when there is a need? Are you trustworthy when someone is counting on you? Do you constantly look for ways to build up the church, or are you critical and fault-finding?

Read Philippians 2:1–5. Do these verses describe your attitude toward other Christians? Circle one.

A. Most of the time

B. Not at all

C. Yes

D. Other _____

Many Christians attend church for what they can get out of it. While it is important to receive spiritual nourishment and encouragement, we must guard against focusing on ourselves.

In what tangible ways can you put the truth of Philippians 2:1–5 into practice?

_____

_____

_____

Do you know another Christian who needs encouragement today? You may want to call that person or write them a card or e-mail. Maybe someone needs help with a problem or an elderly person needs help around her home. Or maybe you know someone who just needs a listening ear. Will you put another's needs and interests above your own?

Reread Philippians 2:5. Fill in the blanks with the missing words.
"Your _____ should be the _____ as that of _____ _____ ."

Wow! I don't know about you, but all too often my attitude is much like the world and very unlike Jesus.

What adjustments do you need to make so that your attitude resembles that of Jesus?

_____

_____

_____

Continue reading Philippians 2:6–8. Jesus was a servant. Priscilla chose to serve as Christ did. One important way that Priscilla served other Christians was by passing on the knowledge that had been given to her. Read Acts 18:24–26.

In what way did Priscilla and Aquila help Apollos? Circle one.
A. Built him a house
B. Gave him money
C. Showed him he was wrong
D. Explained more fully about Christ

Priscilla and Aquila explained to Apollos what they had learned about Jesus. Apollos had only heard what John the Baptist had said about Jesus and didn't know about His life, death, and resurrection. They met with Apollos privately to share the rest of the story. They didn't keep their knowledge to themselves; instead they shared it with those who needed to hear.

Maybe you don't think of yourself as an "expert" in spiritual things, but what you have can be passed along to others. You probably could share wisdom about God with a younger sibling or neighbor. You might consider volunteering with a children's program at your church, or even setting aside a time each day to discuss Jesus with a little brother or sister. You may even have the opportunity to go on a mission trip with your youth group or another group.

In what way will you pass along the knowledge others have given to you?

_____

_____

_____

God never intended for you to be a sponge. He doesn't want you to just receive all the time. He wants you to serve other Christians. Follow the role model of Priscilla and look for opportunities to reach your world with the message of Christ.

Day 4: Serve the Servants

Another important way that Priscilla and her husband Aquila served is by helping ministers. They befriended the apostle Paul and helped him as he carried the truth of Jesus to the nations. Reread Acts 18:1–3.

According to verse 3, in what way did they help Paul? Circle one.
A. Gave money to his ministry
B. Taught him to build tents
C. Let him live with them
D. Taught him about Jesus

Paul was a missionary who traveled from city to city telling people about Jesus Christ. For that reason he didn't have a home, and Priscilla and Aquila took him in. They partnered with him in his work.

List some names of people you know who are in full-time ministry or mission work.

_____

_____

_____

You may have listed your youth minister, pastor, or a missionary. What can you do to help them in their ministry?

_____

_____

_____

Priscilla and Aquila actually worked with Paul and traveled with him to share the gospel. They were probably a constant source of encouragement and support. Think about someone you could support in his or her ministry.

It's so easy for us to think of ministers as superheroes who don't need words of appreciation or help. But did you know that in ministry it's easy to become discouraged and tired? Many ministers simply need a word of thanks. Let's look at three practical ways you can become a Priscilla in someone else's life.

1. Cheer them on.
Read 1 Timothy 5:17. What does this passage teach about those who lead the church?

_____

_____

_____

_____

In what ways can you honor the leaders in your own church? You may want to write one of them a note of thankfulness or perform an act of kindness for him or her. All too often ministry leaders only hear from people who have complaints and criticism. Commit to cheering on one of your leaders today.

2. Help.
Have you ever thought about all the things that happen behind the scenes at your church or youth group? What can you do this week that would help someone in the leadership at your church? Maybe you could donate one afternoon to helping where there is a need. You may offer to stuff envelopes or clean up the church kitchen. You can be sure there are many ways you can help.

And you can also help missionaries and other ministers by giving. Many churches take up missions offerings to support missionaries from their church or denomination. Our money helps provide for missionaries and their ministries. You're not too young to start giving to support missions around the world.

Will you serve someone at your church this week? Circle one.
 A. I don't have time
 B. Maybe

C. Yes

D. Other _____

Will you give financially to help a missionary or missions need you hear about?

A. I don't have any money

B. I'm not sure

C. Yes

D. Other _____

Read Hebrews 6:10. Fill in the blanks with the missing words.

"God is not _____ ; he will not _____ your _____ and the_____ you have shown him as you have _____ his people and _____ to help them."

3. Pray.

While this is often the hardest, it is certainly the most important. Read Paul's own words in Ephesians 6:18–20.

What does he ask the believers to pray for him?

_____

_____

_____

_____

_____

You might want to pick one or two people in ministry to pray for daily. Ask God to give you wisdom in how you should pray for them. You may pick a special Scripture to pray for them or even ask them what their prayer needs are. One great passage to pray is 2 Thessalonians 1:11–12. There are many more throughout the Bible. Ask God to direct you in your prayers for them.

Be a Priscilla in someone's life. Let God make you into the servant that she was.

Day 5: Go Where?

Priscilla and Aquila helped Paul bring the truth of Jesus Christ to those who had never heard about Him. They were some of the first missionaries. Read Acts 18:18. To where did they sail?

Can you remember what they did for a living? (If you can't remember, look back at Acts 18:3.)

_____

_____

_____

They used their profession as a platform for spreading the truth. Their job wasn't only a way to put food on the table; it was a way to invest in God's kingdom. Do you have a job? You may work after school to earn spending money or pay for necessities. If so, have you ever looked at your job as a way to further the name of Jesus? Or maybe you don't work right now. Your "job" is attending school to prepare for your future. Do you see this "job" through the lenses of God's plans?

Do you let Him use you there to draw others to Himself? Circle one.
A. No way
B. Sometimes
C. I want to
D. Other _____

Priscilla and Aquila traveled with Paul to take the gospel to new places. Have you ever considered that one day God might call you to another country in order to share His truth? Read Matthew 28:19–20.

Where does Jesus say we should make disciples?

_____

_____

_____

Did you know that even in our modern world of TV and satellites, many people groups still haven't heard of the love of Jesus? That's hard for many Americans to fathom because we have churches on every corner and Bibles in all translations and styles. But it's true—millions have never heard about Jesus.

If God called you to leave the comfort of your home someday and travel to another country to share His truth, would you go? Why or why not?

_____

_____

_____

Your answer is revealed in the way you live your life today. When He speaks, do you obey? Do you use the witnessing opportunities He gives you? We often think of missionaries as special people who don't like the comfort and safety of America. But missionaries are just like you and me. They just place a higher priority on obeying His call than staying where they are.

We're all called to share the gospel. Some of us will do it in a foreign land. We're all called to surrender our lives. We're all called to follow. For some of us it may mean following down unfamiliar roads.

Read Paul's words in Philippians 3:7–11. How does he consider the things of this world in comparison to knowing Christ? Circle one.
A. Rubbish
  B. Trophies
  C. Foolish
  D. Other _____

Paul knows the truth of Jesus' words in Matthew 16:25. Have you found this verse to be true in your own life? Let go of the things you hold onto and surrender your life to God's plan—whether that's where you are or at the ends of the earth. You can trust your life fully to Him.

Action Point • • • • • • • • • • • • • • • •

This week we studied about letting God use us to minister to others. Take some time to pray about how God wants to use you. Remember, He doesn't want us to be sponges, always taking in and never giving out. Ask God to show you a specific ministry that He wants you to help in at your church. It may be that you go early to your youth group and greet visitors or help your youth minister make copies. Or maybe it's something you've never thought of before. Ask God to show you how He wants you to serve. When He makes it clear, serve there with all your heart.

Leader's Guide

Group Session 1

- Welcome the group.
- Pray for God's guidance.
- Read aloud Mark 5:21–24, 35–43. (Ask a group member to do this.)

Discuss:

1. When circumstances look hopeless, to whom or what do you run? Why?

2. Has there been a time in your life when you were able to trust Jesus and, as Mark 5:36 says, "just believe"? When was it and what happened?

3. What holds you back from believing God? What practical steps can you take to overcome doubt?

4. When did you receive the gift of eternal life? If you haven't yet, what keeps you from doing so?

5. After we are born again, why is it so important to feed ourselves daily meals from God's Word?

6. What's your plan for getting spiritual nourishment daily?

7. If compassion means taking action, how compassionate are you toward those in need?

8. In what ways will you allow God to use you to show others His love and truth?

9. Have you ever kept Jesus' good news a secret? If so, how can you make sure you get the news out?

10. Read Matthew 5:14–16. In what ways can you let your light shine in your school this week?

- Review the memory verse.
- Take prayer requests.
- End with prayer.

Group Session 2

- Welcome the group.
- Pray for God's guidance.
- Read aloud John 4:4–30, 39–42. (Ask group members to take turns.)

Discuss:

1. We are tempted to go to one of three places to get our thirsts met. To which of these places are you most tempted to go?

2. What consequences have you experienced because you went to false wells—or the wrong places—to get your thirsts met?

3. If you see negative patterns in your life, how can you cooperate with God to change those?

4. Read Jeremiah 2:13. Why is it tempting to dig our own wells in order to get our needs met?

5. Why is it important to drink daily from God's Word?

6. Is there a difference in your life when you have a consistent quiet time? If so, describe it.

7. Read Psalm 42:1–2. Discuss the writer's relationship with God. Do you think you'll ever feel the same way in your relationship with God?

8. When you are in a worship setting at church, what steps can you take to help you worship in spirit and truth?

9. How can you build a private worship time into your life?

10. In reading about how Jesus crossed racial boundaries, were you convicted of some changes you need to make? If so, what are they?

- Review memory verse.
- Take prayer requests.
- End with prayer.

Group Session 3

- Welcome the group.
- Pray for God's guidance.
- Read aloud Ruth 2. (Ask group members to take turns.)

Discuss:

1. How did Ruth show she trusted God when she went with Naomi?

2. Describe Ruth's attitude about her singleness. Is your attitude "without a man" like or unlike hers? How?

3. What is more important to you—catching the attention of a guy or pleasing God? Do your actions back up your answer?

4. Do you follow your parents' guidelines regarding relationships with the opposite sex? Why or why not?

5. Read 1 Timothy 5:1. How does flirting contradict what God says about how to treat brothers in Christ?

6. Is it possible to dress modestly and also be in style? Defend your answer.

7. Describe Boaz's character. What qualities do you look for in the guys you date?

8. Review the qualities of a godly man from day 4. Are you willing to not date rather than date someone who doesn't fit this description? Why or why not?

9. From day 5, which of the qualities of a godly woman is the most challenging to you? Why?

10. How can you fall more in love with Jesus? How can you trust Him more with your future?

- Review memory verse.
- Take prayer requests.
- End with prayer.

Group Session 4

- Welcome the group.
- Pray for God's guidance.
- Ask someone to read aloud Luke 10:38–42.

Discuss:

1. Who are you most like, Mary or Martha? Why?

2. What can you do to better listen to God?

3. Reread Luke 10:42. What activities can you eliminate that distract you from focusing on the one thing that is needed?

4. When you spend time alone with God, what difference does it make in your day?

5. What is your most valuable possession? If you felt prompted to, would you let it go for Jesus?

6. Has there ever been a time when following Christ cost you something? If so, describe the situation.

7. Which is more important to you, the opinions of others or pleasing Christ?

8. How can you boldly demonstrate your love for Christ this week?

9. Is Jesus first place in your heart? Explain your answer.

10. What does the way you spend your time say about your love for Christ? How can you carve out more time to spend with Jesus?

- Review memory verse.
- Take prayer requests.
- End with prayer.

Group Session 5

- Welcome the group.
- Pray for God's leading.
- Ask group members to read aloud John 8:1–11.

Discuss:

1. How do you think the woman felt when she was dragged in front of the crowd?

2. Why is it so hard to break the power of habitual sin? Is there any hope for overcoming?

3. Read 1 John 1:9. Explain what this promise means.

4. When you sin, do you act on this promise? Why or why not?

5. Read Hebrews 12:9–11. In what ways is God's discipline different from that of our earthly parents?

6. Has there ever been a time when the Lord disciplined you? If so, what did you learn?

7. Read 2 Corinthians 10:5. How can you learn to do this?

8. What tempting situations do you put yourself in that you need to avoid?

9. How can you live like the "new creation" the Bible says you are?

10. Is there someone who knows your struggles and can pray for you and hold you accountable? If not, will you find somebody who can?

- Review memory verse.
- Take prayer requests.
- End with prayer.

Group Session 6

- Welcome the group.
- Pray for God's guidance.
- Read aloud 2 Samuel 13:1–19. (Ask group members to take turns.)

Discuss:

1. Do your friends encourage you to make wise choices or do they tempt you to compromise?

2. What kind of friend are you? If a friend is headed for trouble, do you speak the truth in love to them?

3. Read 1 Corinthians 13:4–8. What are the differences between love and lust?

4. Which is most often portrayed in movies and music, love or lust? Defend your answer.

5. Read Psalm 147:3–5. What hope does this passage give for those who are hurting?

6. How does being open with God and others about our pain start the healing process?

7. Why is God's Word crucial in healing from serious wounds?

8. Do you believe it's possible for God to restore wholeness to someone after they've been wounded deeply? Read Joel 2:25 and discuss what it means.

9. Has God ever used a tragedy in your life to bring good out of it for you and others?

10. Read Jeremiah 29:11. How does this promise apply to your own life?

- Review memory verse.
- Take prayer requests.
- End with prayer.

Group Session 7

- Welcome the group.
- Pray for God's guidance.
- Read aloud Luke 1:26-45. (Ask several members to take turns.)

Discuss:

1. If you had been in Mary's shoes, how would you have responded?

2. Read 2 Chronicles 16:9. Would you say that your heart is fully committed to Him? Why or why not?

3. What are some of the benefits of having a spiritual mentor in your life?

4. Do you have a mentor? If not, are you willing to find one?

5. Does Luke 1:45 describe you? Why or why not?

6. Read Romans 10:17. What connection does the Word of God have with believing God?

7. Read aloud Luke 1:46–55. What are some of the things that Mary praised God for?

8. What are some things that you can praise God for?

9. Read Psalm 139:13–16. Do you believe that God created you with a special plan for your life?

10. Are you willing to surrender your own plans to God if He asks you to? Will you trust God with your life?

- Review memory verse.
- Take prayer requests.
- End with prayer.

Group Session 8

- Welcome the group.
- Pray for God's guidance.
- Read aloud Esther 4. (Ask several members to take turns.)

Discuss:

1. How would you have felt if you were Esther and were suddenly made queen?

2. Describe how Esther treated her cousin Mordecai.

3. Read Acts 5:29. Have you ever had to choose between obeying God and man? If so, describe the situation.

4. What positions have you been placed in "for such a time as this"? How will you let God use you?

5. Have you ever risked anything in order to stand up for what was right? Describe what happened.

6. Is God calling you to take a stand for Him in a certain situation? If so, what is it?

7. In what ways has God prepared you in the past to stand up for Him in the present?

8. Has there ever been a time when you stepped out in faith and were blessed as a result?

9. Are you more focused on outer beauty or inner character qualities? Be honest.

10. Review the list of qualities in Day 5. What quality do you most want God to develop in you?

- Review the memory verse.
- Take prayer requests.
- End with prayer.

Group Session 9

- Welcome the group.
- Pray for God's guidance.
- Read aloud Numbers 12:1–15. (Have group members take turns.)

Discuss:

1. Read Exodus 2:4–8. What do we learn about Miriam from this passage?

2. How seriously do you take your role to protect your younger siblings or neighbors?

3. Review the list of leadership qualities from Day 2. Which one do you think is the most important? Why?

4. The best leaders are Christ followers. Explain this statement.

5. Read James 3:9–10. What is the biggest struggle you have in regard to your tongue? What can you do to overcome this?

6. How can we remind ourselves that the Lord is listening to every conversation? Do you think that would help us control our words?

7. Read Romans 13:1–2. When we rebel against our authorities, what does the Bible say we're really doing?

8. What consequences have you suffered because you rebelled against authority? What changes did you make after that experience?

9. Read Psalm 86:5. What do we learn about God's grace through the life of Miriam?

10. What can you do to avoid some of the mistakes Miriam made?

- Review the memory verse.
- Take prayer requests.
- End with prayer.

Group Session 10

- Welcome the group.
- Pray for God's guidance.
- Read aloud 1 Samuel 1:9-28. (Ask several group members to read.)

Discuss:

1. When you're sad, do you bring your needs to the Lord? Why or why not?

2. Can you recall a time when you experienced peace after praying about a problem or need? Describe the situation.

3. Read Matthew 6:8. Explain why we pray if God already knows our needs.

4. Have you ever received a "no" answer to a prayer and later seen how God worked it out for your good? If so, explain.

5. Read 1 Samuel 1:27–28. Have you ever surrendered something to God that you loved dearly? If so, what was it?

6. Read Ecclesiastes 5:4–5. Why is it important that we take seriously the words we speak to God?

7. When God answers your prayers, do you thank Him or forget you prayed in the first place?

8. Read Philippians 4:11. Have you learned contentment in the Lord no matter what answers to prayer you receive?

9. What is the biggest obstacle you face in deepening your prayer life? How can you overcome this?

10. Read 1 Thessalonians 5:17. Explain what this means and how to put it into practice in your daily life.

- Review the memory verse.
- Take prayer requests.
- End with prayer.

Group Session 11

- Welcome the group.
- Pray for God's guidance.
- Ask a group member to read Romans 16:1–2.

Discuss:

1. Would others describe you the same way Paul described Phoebe in this passage? Why or why not?

2. List women you know who God has used to minister to others. What characteristics do they all have in common?

3. Read John 13:12–17. In what ways can you wash others' feet as Jesus washed His disciples' feet?

4. Read Malachi 3:10. What does the way we handle our money show about our trust in God?

5. Explain the difference between having self-confidence and confidence in God. Which is more beneficial? Why?

6. Read Ephesians 4:1. What does a "life worthy of the calling you have received" mean? What can you do to make sure you're living your life this way?

7. Read James 1:22–25. Explain the difference between hearing the Word and acting on the Word. Is there an area of your life where you need to move from hearing to action?

8. Describe how you have changed as a result of studying and applying God's Word to a certain situation.

9. Read 1 Corinthians 12:14–20. Describe how the different people in the body of Christ work together to accomplish God's work.

10. Do you view yourself as someone whom God wants to use in the world? Why or why not?

- Review the memory verse.
- Take prayer requests.
- End with prayer.

Group Session 12

- Welcome the group.
- Pray for God's guidance.
- Read aloud Acts 18:1–3.

Discuss:

1. Have you ever been persecuted or excluded because of your faith? Describe the situation.

2. Read 2 Timothy 3:12. What does this verse mean for your own life? How will you handle persecution?

3. Read Romans 16:3–4. Have you ever risked anything for the cause of Christ? If so, what was it?

4. Read 2 Corinthians 6:14–16. Describe Priscilla and Aquila's relationship. Would this have been possible if one of them had not been a believer?

5. Read Philippians 2:1–5. In what way can you apply this verse in how you treat fellow believers?

6. How can you pass on what you've learned about God to others?

7. In what ways have you committed to serve in your church or youth group?

8. What one leader or minister in your church are you committed to pray for?

9. Read Matthew 28:19–20. If God called you to another country to share His love, would you go?

10. Read Philippians 3:7. Can you honestly say that you, like Paul, count the things of this world as loss for the sake of Christ? Why or why not?

- Review the memory verse.
- Take prayer requests.
- End with prayer